THE COMPLETE IDIOT'S GUIDE™ TO

eBay Motors

by Lissa McGrath

ALPHA

A member of Penguin Group (USA) Inc.

ALPHA BOOKS

Published by the Penguin Group

Penguin Group (USA) Inc., 375 Hudson Street, New York, New York 10014, USA

Penguin Group (Canada), 90 Eglinton Avenue East, Suite 700, Toronto, Ontario M4P 2Y3, Canada (a division of Pearson Penguin Canada Inc.)

Penguin Books Ltd., 80 Strand, London WC2R 0RL, England

Penguin Ireland, 25 St. Stephen's Green, Dublin 2, Ireland (a division of Penguin Books Ltd.)

Penguin Group (Australia), 250 Camberwell Road, Camberwell, Victoria 3124, Australia (a division of Pearson Australia Group Pty. Ltd.)

Penguin Books India Pvt. Ltd., 11 Community Centre, Panchsheel Park, New Delhi—110 017, India

Penguin Group (NZ), 67 Apollo Drive, Rosedale, North Shore, Auckland 1311, New Zealand (a division of Pearson New Zealand Ltd.)

Penguin Books (South Africa) (Pty.) Ltd., 24 Sturdee Avenue, Rosebank, Johannesburg 2196, South Africa

Penguin Books Ltd., Registered Offices: 80 Strand, London WC2R 0RL, England

International Standard Book Number: 978-1-59257-758-3
Library of Congress Catalog Card Number: 2007941484

10   09   08   8   7   6   5   4   3   2   1

Interpretation of the printing code: The rightmost number of the first series of numbers is the year of the book's printing; the rightmost number of the second series of numbers is the number of the book's printing. For example, a printing code of 08-1 shows that the first printing occurred in 2008.

Printed in the United States of America

Contents

Introduction

There are very few people who have not heard of eBay. It is the largest online marketplace where people gather to buy and sell new and used items.

In 2000, eBay decided that because there were so many sellers of vehicles, parts, and accessories on eBay, they would create an entirely new site for them. Thus, eBay Motors was born.

Since then, more than 2 million passenger vehicles have been sold through eBay Motors on the United States site alone. That's not to mention the millions of parts and accessories. If it has a motor, or relates to something that does, you'll likely find it on eBay Motors.

eBay Motors is distinctly different from eBay itself, so there are different tips, tricks, pitfalls, and red flags to look for. There are many additional features, too, including a comprehensive fraud protection program, exclusive to eBay Motors.

Whether you're a buyer, private-party seller, vehicle dealer, or strictly only sell parts and accessories, this book shows you step by step how to be successful on eBay Motors right from day one.

Extras

Along with the book being separated into two parts, "eBay Motors for Buyers" and "eBay Motors for Sellers," I provide you with some extra tidbits of information to help you navigate eBay Motors with ease.

def•i•ni•tion

These explain some eBay terms as well as eBay Motors terms.

Check Engine

These are warnings about legalities and ways to prevent problems and protect yourself while enjoying your eBay Motors experiences.

Detailing Tips

These are short, practical tips of things I have discovered during my years working with eBay Motors.

Driver's Ed

These give extra information that might be of interest to you.

Acknowledgments

Thank you to Tom Stevens and Nancy Lewis for their continued support and expertise. It's always a pleasure working with you both. Also thank you to my agent, Marilyn Allen, for her encouragement and expert assistance in all things book-related.

To Steve Lindhorst, a big thank you for taking on the technical review. Steve, your expertise is always appreciated, and this book is definitely better for your input.

And finally, to my husband Chris and wonderful daughter Rowan. You are the two biggest joys in my life and the reason I love what I do.

Special Thanks to the Technical Reviewer

The Pocket Idiot's Guide to eBay Motors was reviewed by an expert who double-checked the accuracy of what you'll learn here, to help us ensure that this book gives you everything you need to know about buying and selling vehicles and parts online. Special thanks are extended to Steve Lindhorst.

Steve Lindhorst is a nationally recognized expert on eBay Motors. Previously an eBay employee, he is one of only a handful of instructors for eBay's own eBay University on the national level. Steve has been instructing eBay University classes for eBay and eBay Motors since 2002, he has listed and sold hundreds of vehicles, and he has taught hundreds of auto dealers across the United States how to leverage the power of eBay Motors for additional sales. Learn more about Steve by visiting www. DealerClasses.com.

Trademarks

All terms mentioned in this book that are known to be or are suspected of being trademarks or service marks have been appropriately capitalized. Alpha

eBay Motors for Buyers

eBay Motors is the number-one automotive site on the web. If you're looking for a vehicle, parts, accessories, or even an interesting birthday present for a "car nut" friend, the place to look is eBay Motors.

Throughout these first six chapters, we look at how to buy on eBay Motors, how to find a real bargain, and the red flags to watch out for. After you've read this part, you'll know everything you need to know about being a savvy buyer on eBay Motors.

What Is eBay Motors?

In This Chapter

- What is eBay Motors and why should I use it?
- What can I buy on eBay Motors?
- Getting registered for eBay and PayPal
- An introduction to safety and fraud protection on eBay Motors

Many people think eBay Motors is a relatively new site. But it's actually been around for seven years and has shown an excellent track record over that time.

eBay Motors was launched in 2000 after eBay realized that it needed a dedicated area for the thousands of sellers trading vehicles and parts on eBay.com.

Here are some facts about eBay Motors that you may not know:

- Twelve million unique visitors shop on eBay Motors every month.
- In the third quarter of 2007, the total sales for eBay Motors (worldwide) was $17.9 billion.

- More than 2 million passenger vehicles have been sold on eBay Motors in the United States alone.

- Also in the third quarter of 2007, approximately 1 million parts and accessories were available for sale at any given time on eBay Motors (United States).

- Approximately 70 percent of vehicles sold on eBay Motors are delivered to buyers outside of the seller's state.

- A passenger vehicle is sold on eBay Motors every minute.

- A motorcycle is sold on eBay Motors every three minutes.

- A part or accessory is sold on eBay Motors every second.

- As well as private-party sellers, approximately 15,000 dealers now sell on eBay Motors.

These are pretty impressive stats, considering that eBay Motors was an "add-on" to eBay's main site.

eBay Motors also has its own URL, www.motors. eBay.com, but most people go to www.eBay.com first and then click on the Motors link.

Registration

If you're already registered for eBay, you do not have to register again for eBay Motors. If you're not already an eBay user, registration is very easy:

1. Go to www.ebay.com.
2. Click Register at the top of the page.
3. Fill out the registration form.

As well as your name and address, you'll also need to enter a valid phone number. If eBay discovers that the number is invalid, your account could be suspended, so be sure to keep that up-to-date.

You'll need to select a User ID. Because there are around 250 million eBay users (and growing), you need to get a bit creative. I suggest you don't use your own name for security reasons. But other than that, anything goes. If you're in business, you might want to choose something that reflects what you sell, such as junkyard_gems, theperfectride, or crazyaboutcorvettes. Dealerships often use their business name to build credibility.

There are some restrictions to characters you can and cannot use in your User ID. You can read them all at pages.ebay.com/help/newtoebay/user_id.html. If you stick to underscores or the * character, you will be fine.

To finish your registration you'll need to set up a password and secret question. Make your password secure by using a combination of uppercase and lowercase letters and numbers, and don't set your computer to automatically remember it—that defeats the purpose of having a password in the first place.

After you finish the registration form, eBay will send you a confirmation e-mail (to be sure the e-mail address you entered is valid). Click on the confirmation link, and you're done!

Why and When You Need to Get Verified

Getting verified simply means you've added a credit or debit card to your eBay account to verify your identity. You may be prompted to get verified during the registration process if your e-mail address is a free account (Hotmail, Yahoo!, etc.). You will also need to get verified if you want to place a bid over $15,000 or if you want to become a seller.

The verification process is fairly simple. You start in *My eBay*.

def•i•ni•tion

My eBay is the hub of all of your eBay activity. Here you will find all your current and past transactions (watching, bought, selling, sold, etc.). You also access your eBay e-mail account (called My Messages) through My eBay.

1. Click the My eBay tab in the top right navigation bar of the page.
2. Click Personal Information. (It's under the My Account heading on the left sidebar.)
3. Scroll down to the Financial Information section, and click Edit next to the Credit Card Details.

4. Follow the prompts to enter your credit or debit card information. (Your card won't be charged.)

5. As long as the name and address information matches your eBay registration information, you are now verified.

If you don't have a credit or debit card (or don't want to use it) you can become *ID Verified* instead.

def•i•ni•tion

> **ID Verify** confirms your identity by asking you questions from your credit history.

Questions you may be asked include the range of your monthly mortgage payment, your loan holder for a particular loan, etc. A credit inquiry is run to generate these questions, but this does not count as a "hit" on your credit. The service costs $5 and is valid until you change your address or phone number.

The fee is charged to your eBay account, so you pay for it using any of the payment methods eBay accepts (bank transfer, check, PayPal, credit/debit card, etc.).

PayPal for Buyers

PayPal is an online payment processing company that enables you to pay a seller with your credit card or a bank account transfer without divulging your financial information. Sellers may pay fees for receiving the payment, but buyers are never charged for their account.

To set up a PayPal account, go to www.PayPal.com and click Sign Up. It's a pretty self-explanatory process, so just follow the prompts.

After you set up your account, you need to add a bank account to be able to send payments. I recommend you also add a credit card because it will enable instant transfers even when your PayPal account balance doesn't cover the full payment amount. This way the seller gets the full payment instantly and can ship the item to you without waiting for the bank account transfer to clear. If there are insufficient funds in your bank account, PayPal debits your credit card instead.

It takes a couple days to add a bank account because you have to wait for two small deposits from PayPal to show up in your bank account. You then verify these to confirm that you are the account holder.

What Sells on eBay Motors?

It really goes without saying that you'll find cars, trucks, and motorcycles on eBay Motors, but there's so much more to be found there.

In fact, the most expensive item ever sold on eBay was listed on eBay Motors. It was a 405-foot steel yacht nicknamed the "Gigayacht" sold for $85 million. This sale trumped the previous most expensive item, which was a $4.9 million Gulfstream II jet.

But it's not all million-dollar aircraft and vessels. There are plenty of affordable vehicles on eBay Motors, including ATVs, go-karts, scooters/mopeds, snowmobiles, boats, aircraft, buses, commercial trucks, military vehicles, race cars, RVs/campers, trailers, and powersports (jet-skis, etc.).

Don't forget that there are also over a million parts and accessories listings at any one time on eBay Motors. You can find parts and upgrades for your vehicle as well as collectibles, apparel, key chains, die-cast models, and pretty much anything else you can think of that an enthusiast of that particular vehicle could ever want.

How Safe Is eBay Motors?

eBay has many fraud-protection tools, such as masking bidder User IDs when the bid price is over $200, using My Messages for e-mail communication, requiring users to sign in again at least once a day, plus a whole host of "back-end" fraud-detection tools.

However, this is not a replacement for general common sense. There are 247 million eBay users. It's very difficult for eBay to police all of them all of the time. So it's up to you to follow safe trading practices.

The following are 10 tips for safe trading on eBay Motors:

1. Never buy from a seller off eBay (you lose your fraud protection).

2. Never pay for an auction through a cash transfer service (Western Union, MoneyGram, etc.). I talk about safe payment methods in Chapter 4.

3. Always check the seller's feedback and be wary of new users, those with only feedback as buyers, or those with low feedback ratings.

4. Request the seller's contact information through eBay before you send a payment to be sure it matches the information he or she gives you.

5. Get a vehicle history report through AutoCheck or CARFAX.

6. If you have any questions, ask them *before* you bid.

7. Never buy a vehicle from an overseas seller (even if he or she offers you free shipping).

8. If possible, inspect the vehicle yourself, or get a certified inspection performed for you before you bid.

9. Know the retail and private-party value for the vehicle. If it's priced significantly lower, there's usually a reason.

10. Trust your instincts. If a deal looks too good to be true, it probably is.

I elaborate on many of those points throughout this book, but as long as you follow these basic practices, you should be fine. However, if something does go wrong, eBay offers specific fraud protection for eBay Motors buyers, which I address in Chapter 6.

The Least You Need to Know

- Choose a User ID that reflects you, but don't use your full name for security reasons.
- You have to get verified if you want to bid over $15,000.
- Register for PayPal and add both a credit card and bank account to get access to instant transfers for every transaction.
- You can find almost any type of motorized vehicle on eBay Motors, plus parts, accessories, and collectibles.

Finding Your Perfect Ride

In This Chapter

- Finding vehicles by browsing, searching, or both
- Finding local vehicles
- How to read the search results page
- Narrowing down the results to the exact specs of your perfect ride
- What you should look for on the auction page

As of this writing, more than 65,000 vehicle listings are on eBay Motors (plus more than 1.17 million parts and accessories). Finding the one perfect vehicle for you among that many listings sounds like a daunting task. If you were reading through the car ads in a newspaper, you'd have to read every single one. Thankfully, eBay is set up a little differently and you can narrow down results by browsing specific vehicle types, makes, or models, or by searching for the exact vehicle you want.

In this chapter, we look at what eBay calls "finding." It encompasses both browsing and searching.
By the end of this chapter, you'll know exactly how
to find what you're looking for on eBay Motors.

To Search or Not to Search?

eBay redesigned eBay Motors recently. In fact, as
of this writing, it is still in the final testing stages.
However, eBay is allowing access to the beta site,
so I'll discuss the new site rather than the old one.
If the top bar looks like the following figure, then
eBay has finished its launch of the new site design
and you will automatically see everything as I discuss it in this book.

The new eBay Motors design.

However, if it looks like the following figure, then
you are still seeing the old design and will need to
go to the beta site (www.playground.eBay.com) and
click on the Motors tab to see the new design. This
is still an active site, so all bids are binding.

The old eBay Motors design.

Browsing by Make and Model

If you know the vehicle you are looking for, the simplest way to find it is to use the Make and Model drop-down menus. You can use the search box if you prefer, but that brings up all items on eBay Motors that use those words. So you get a lot of generic parts and accessories as well as the vehicles. Using the drop-down menus takes you to the specific category for that make and model, and only displays actual vehicles for sale.

If you're looking for parts and accessories for a particular vehicle, you can click the Parts and Accessories tab and enter the make, model, year, and a keyword for the part name to go directly to those items. Using the menus prevents you getting listings for the actual vehicle rather than parts.

Browsing by Vehicle Type

If you're looking for powersports, motorcycles, or boats, use the tab at the top of the page to go to that specific category. If you're looking for something that doesn't fit into any of those categories, nor Parts and Accessories or Cars and Trucks, the chances are it will be covered in the Other Vehicles section. There is a tab for that category, too. If you're not sure, hover your mouse over the tab to bring up a menu showing the main categories within that section. If you click on one of these categories, you'll go straight to the results page. If you just click on the main tab, you'll go to a page where you can specialize further and see all the subcategories within these categories.

You can locate a car or truck by type from the Cars and Trucks tab on the main eBay Motors page. Select the icons representing the vehicle type you want. The options are sedan, minivan, coupe, convertible, wagon, SUV, truck, alternative fuel, and collector car.

You can then narrow down the results by Year Range, Mileage, Engine, and Make. This is a really useful feature when you don't really know exactly what you want.

Searching Using Keywords

If you prefer searching to browsing, you can enter keywords into the search box at the top of the page. This returns all listings with those keywords, whether it's parts, accessories, or actual vehicles.

You can exclude words by placing a minus sign right before the word. So *350z -manual* brings up listings that have the word "350z" but do not have the word "manual" in their title.

This is reliant on the seller putting the right keywords in his 55-character title. For example, not every 350z seller will have the keyword "manual" or "automatic" in the title.

I have found that on eBay Motors, it's easier to get into the right general category before searching. Other tools on the search results page help you narrow down the results, too.

The Search Results Page

There are a lot of features and options on this page, and the best way you can get comfortable and familiar with it is to use it. However, here are some of the highlights, including new features eBay has recently introduced.

Features Specific to Make/Model Category Pages	
What It's Worth	The price range of this vehicle recently sold on eBay Motors and the Kelley Blue Book retail range
Number for Sale	The number of active listings for this vehicle and current bid price range
Tabs across the page	Vehicles for Sale (listing results)
	Specs & Photos (stock information)
	Ratings & Reviews (from eBay members)
	Price Research (from Kelley Blue Book)
	Parts & Accessories (listings in the Parts & Accessories category for this specific make and model)
Save Vehicle	Option to keep track of vehicle models you are interested in (not the actual listings themselves)

In a moment we'll look at how to narrow down the results, but first let's look at what you can see about the vehicle from the results page. Each listing shows:

- Thumbnail gallery picture
- Listing title
- Model year
- Mileage on vehicle
- Number of bids so far
- Current price
- Time left
- Watch this item button (to add the listing to your watched items list in My eBay)

Some have borders around the title and picture, others show the title text in boldface, and others may have a shaded background color. These are all upgrade features the seller paid for to make his or her listing stand out. It does not mean that those items are any better than any other item.

Types of Auctions

There are four types of listings you'll see on the main search results page on eBay Motors:

Online Auction. Highest bidder at the end of the set duration wins the item.

Buy It Now Fixed Price. The Buy It Now price is the only price (i.e., there is no bidding). When a buyer clicks Buy It Now, the listing ends immediately and that buyer wins the item.

Buy It Now Auction. Has both a starting price (like the online auction) and a fixed price. If a buyer places a bid (rather than paying the higher Buy It Now price), the Buy It Now option disappears and the auction then runs its term as an online auction. However, if the first bidder chooses to use the Buy It Now option, the auction ends immediately, and the item is sold to that bidder at the fixed price.

Best Offer. Used in conjunction with a Buy It Now Fixed Price Listing. Bidders can offer a lower "best offer" price to the seller. This can be accepted, countered, or rejected. It's always worth submitting a Best Offer because the seller is expecting to sell the item for less than the Buy It Now price. You may have to haggle, but that's part of the fun.

There is one exception to the Buy It Now Auction. If there is a *Reserve Price* set on the auction, then the Buy It Now price only disappears after the bidding has reached the reserve. Until that time, any future bidders can use the Buy It Now option.

def•i•ni•tion

A **Reserve Price** is the minimum amount the seller is willing to sell the item for. It's hidden from buyer's view and is usually much higher than the starting price.

You can see if an auction has a reserve price by looking for the words "Reserve not met" beneath the current bid. If this is not there, either there was no reserve, or it has already been met.

Right now eBay is testing keeping the Buy It Now option active even after the first bid is placed on all Buy It Now auctions (with or without a Reserve Price). Parts and Accessories is one of the test categories.

Even if the Reserve Price is not met, a seller may send an unsuccessful bidder a *Second Chance Offer*. Second Chance Offers are completely optional for both buyers and sellers. If you receive one and are not willing to pay that price, either decline it or just let it expire (usually within 24 to 48 hours).

def•i•ni•tion _____

A **Second Chance Offer** is an offer to purchase an item you bid on but did not win.

eBay Motors is the only place a seller may modify the Second Chance Offer price. On the rest of eBay, the offer is for the maximum bid from that bidder. However, on eBay Motors, the seller may increase the Second Chance Offer amount up to (but not exceeding) the Reserve Price. The bidder doesn't have to accept it, though.

Featured Items

I mentioned title upgrades (bold, highlight, border, etc.) a moment ago. There is another upgrade the seller can pay for, called Featured Plus. This puts the seller's listing ahead of all the other items on that page. So if you have the list sorted by Time: Ending Soonest, the top items will be the featured ones, even if there are nonfeatured items that end sooner. You can see where the featured items end and the regular listings begin by looking for a line across the page and the text "learn how to promote your items" written above it.

Driver's Ed

You can sort the listing results by time remaining on the auction, price, distance, model year, or mileage.

Many buyers don't look past the featured items so they don't realize that there are other items ending sooner that may be a lower price. So to find a good deal, don't forget to look at the nonfeatured items.

Narrow Down Your Results

I mentioned earlier that you can limit the search results after you've already reached the results page. Here's how you do it.

At the top of the Vehicles for Sale tab, you'll see a variety of options. These vary based on the vehicle. Let's use Ford Mustang as an example. The options here are *Generation*, Model Year, Transmission, and Condition.

def•i•ni•tion

> Each time the manufacturer redesigns the car but keeps the same model name, it is identified as a new **Generation** of that model.

Each option under those headings has a number next to it. That tells you how many listings match when you select that option.

Using our Ford Mustang example, if you limit the results to Generation: 2005–Current, the number of relevant listings goes from 1,541 to 399. Now, if you select Manual for the Transmission, that takes it down to 289. Select Used Condition, and you've narrowed it down to 145.

By this stage, you've used up most of the original options, so eBay adds in other options like Exterior Color, Fuel Type, etc. These are always accessible through the More Options to Browse section that displays as links below the original options.

Other options include Interior Color, Body Type, Number of Cylinders, Price, Type of Vehicle Title, Buying Options (PayPal or Buy It Now), and Distance (from your zip code).

By limiting the results, one at a time, you can get to the relevant listings very quickly. Try doing that at a dealership!

The Auction Listing Page

On the item page you'll see …

- A set of tabs across the page labeled Seller's Description, History Report, Shipping, Financing, and Buyer Checklist. (We're only looking at the first tab in this chapter. The others will come later.)

- A box with information about the seller (called Meet the Seller), which I discuss in Chapter 3.

- An Item Specifics section that covers all the major details of the vehicle. This is where eBay pulls the data from you used to narrow down the results.

- The Vehicle Description that the seller wrote. This should cover all the extra details and options not included in the Item Specifics (you'll probably see some overlap) plus a good number of photographs of the exterior and interior. You might also see an embedded video of the car.

- The Shipping, Payment Details, and Return Policy section.

- The box to enter your bid.

These sections should be pretty self-explanatory. Some sellers write better descriptions than others. Likewise, photographs may be better from some sellers. You always have the option to Ask Seller a Question using the link in the Meet the Seller box. If you're unsure of something, or the description doesn't explain something explicitly, don't assume, ask. This is too expensive an item to not have all the information at your fingertips.

The Least You Need to Know

- The easiest way to find a car or truck is to use the drop-down menu to navigate to the Make/Model category and then narrow down results from there.

- You can choose how to limit the results based on your own preferences.

- Featured items display before regular listings on each results page, so scroll down past the separation line to find auctions that have less visibility (and often fewer bids and lower prices).

- Sellers use Reserve Prices so they can start the bidding low to build interest, but still protect themselves from selling the vehicle for less than they want.

Avoiding PBB (Post-Bidder Blues)

In This Chapter

- Investigating the seller before you bid
- Inspections, vehicle history reports, and other tools for researching the vehicle
- How to decide how much to bid
- Watch out for hidden terms or fees

You've narrowed down the results to a manageable size and found a few auctions that you're really interested in. Now you need to do your research. Post-bidder blues, buyer's remorse—whatever you want to call it—can happen in any auction. However, when you're laying out the kind of money that changes hands on eBay Motors, you really need to be 100 percent certain before you bid.

eBay gives you some great tools to help with this. Some are exclusive to eBay Motors; others you will have seen on other areas of eBay. By using these wisely, you're also helping protect yourself from fraud and other seller issues. Fraud-protection services are great (I talk about those in Chapters 4 and 6), but they are no substitute for common sense and pre-bidding research.

When you reach the end of this chapter, you'll know how to use all of the research tools savvy eBay Motors buyers use for every purchase.

Researching the Seller

In Chapter 2, I mentioned the Meet the Seller box on the auction listing page. This gives you a snapshot of the seller's history on eBay. This information is based on transactions on all of eBay, not just eBay Motors.

The first line tells you the seller's User ID and then gives you his or her *feedback score* in parentheses next to it.

def•i•ni•tion

The **feedback score** is calculated based on the total number of unique feedback comments given to a user. A positive comment is assigned +1, and a negative comment −1. Neutral feedback comments are assigned a 0 value.

The feedback score totals only unique feedback, so only one comment from each eBay user counts. So if a buyer purchases five items from a seller and leaves five positive feedback comments for

him, they only actually count as +1 for the feedback score. If a seller receives 150 unique positive
feedback comments and 3 negative comments, his
feedback score would be 147 (150 positive minus 3
negative).

If the seller has a feedback score of 10 or more,
there will be a star next to the feedback score.
This changes color as the seller's feedback score
increases. After an eBay user gets a feedback
score of 10,000, the star becomes a shooting star.

Next to the star you may see one of many different
icons.

Seller's User ID Icons

me	About Me page	A page about the seller and/or his business.
⊻	ID Verified	This user's identity has been confirmed.
⧄	Changed User ID	This user has changed his or her User ID within the last 30 days.
⧄	New Member	This user registered on eBay within the last 30 days.
Power Seller	PowerSeller	An experienced seller with a high positive feedback rating. The PowerSeller must maintain $1,000 mini-mum in sales or 100 items sold per month to keep PowerSeller status.

continues

continued

Seller's User ID Icons

	eBay Store	This seller manages an eBay Store of fixed-price Buy It Now items. Parts and Accessories sellers often have an eBay Store.

Next, you'll see the feedback rating. This is different from the feedback score because it shows the percentage of all feedback comments received that were positive. It is based on all feedback received, not just one per user. PowerSellers are required to maintain a 98 percent positive feedback rating. So to keep their PowerSeller status, 98 out of every 100 feedback comments they receive must be positive.

In general, you should watch out for sellers with a feedback rating lower than 97 percent positive. But you should still check the actual comments to see what they were, and see how many negatives are actually affecting the rating.

The line below the feedback rating shows how long the seller has been an eBay member. This does not tell you how long he or she has been actively selling though. You'll need to look at the feedback profile to see that. This line also shows you which country the seller is registered in. So if you think you're buying a part from Ohio and the seller is registered in China, you might be in for a surprise in terms of quality, who actually made the part, and delivery time. For eBay Motors purchases, I strongly recommend that you stick to sellers who are registered in the United States, or possibly Canada.

Why Is Feedback Important?

When you drive down "car dealer row" in your town, you can easily identify dealerships that you don't want to buy from. Appearance means a lot. Online, it's harder for buyers to spot "dodgy" dealerships because most dealership listings look similar. So it's important to look at their feedback.

Think about car dealer row again for a moment. What if every buyer came back a month or so after buying their car and left a comment about the dealership for all potential buyers to see? If you were considering buying from this dealer, you'd be pretty crazy not to read those comments. On eBay, you have comments from literally thousands of previous buyers and *Detailed Seller Ratings* that show you a breakdown of how the seller performed in various aspects of the sale.

def•i•ni•tion

Detailed Seller Ratings are an anonymous score from 1 to 5 that a buyer can give the seller for different aspects of the transaction.

If you pay attention to the feedback, it doesn't matter how fancy or flashy the "dealership" looks. You will know the truth behind the smoke and mirrors.

Interpreting the Feedback Profile

On the next line in the Meet the Seller box is a link to See Detailed Feedback. This takes you straight to the seller's feedback profile.

Detailing Tips

I can't stress how important it is to read the information on the feedback profile. The snapshot you get from the Meet the Seller box is great at helping you spot red flags (non-U.S. seller, recently registered, low feedback, etc.), but it doesn't give you all the information you need to know to make an informed decision about a seller.

On the feedback profile you'll see the breakdown of the feedback numbers, which includes the total number of positive feedback (i.e., including repeat buyers). A high number of repeat buyers shows that buyers liked the transaction and came back for more.

To the right, you'll see the Recent Feedback Ratings box. This shows you how much of the feedback is from transactions within the last month, 6 months, and 12 months.

If a seller has negative feedback, but none within the last 12 months, you can assume that he or she fixed whatever the problem was. However, if there are a string of negative feedbacks in the last month or six months, you should be more wary of this seller, and definitely read those comments to see what the problem was.

Detailed Seller Ratings

Whenever a buyer leaves feedback, he or she has the opportunity to leave an anonymous 1 to 5 rating for the seller based on four criteria:

- Item as described
- Communication
- Shipping time
- Shipping and handling charges

These are called Detailed Seller Ratings. For vehicle sellers, you won't see the bottom two options because it is the buyer's responsibility to arrange shipping.

This is an optional feature, so not all buyers use it, and it is based on only the last 12 months' worth of ratings.

Seller Versus Buyer Feedback

When you look at the actual feedback comments, you'll see that the default tab is Feedback as Seller. There are also tabs for Feedback as Buyer, All Feedback, and Feedback Left for Others. Feedback as a Buyer is important because it shows the seller has experience on both sides of the transaction; however, the Feedback as Seller is far more important (hence being the default view). It's also worth checking out the Feedback Left for Others to see what you can expect if you do complete a transaction with this seller.

Within each comment line you'll see (from left to right):

- A colored icon showing whether the comment was positive (green), negative (red), or neutral (gray).
- The feedback comment left by the other user.
- The User ID of the person leaving the feedback comment and his or her feedback rating.
- The date and time the comment was left.

For transactions where this user was the seller, the listing title for the item that was sold will display below the feedback comment and also the final price the buyer paid (excluding shipping). This makes it much easier to check that you have a seller with real experience rather than someone who's *feedback farming*.

def•i•ni•tion _____

> **Feedback farming** is when a new seller sells very cheap items (such as e-books for a penny), to build up their feedback rating. Scammers often try to use this tactic to make themselves look more credible.

You'll only be able to see the auction title and price for 90 days. Then you'll just see the comment and the date.

Red Flags to Watch Out For

These are the red flags to watch out for when looking at a seller's feedback:

- Recently registered on eBay
- Seller is not registered in either the United
  States or Canada
- Changed User ID within the last 30 days
- Low feedback score
- Ninety-seven percent positive feedback rat-
  ing or lower
- Little or no feedback as the seller
- Feedback as the seller is limited to very
  cheap items unrelated to eBay Motors
- Detailed Seller Ratings are below three stars
  for any one criterion

If you see one of these, you need to be a bit more
careful. More than one is a big warning against
this seller. If you see three or more, go back to the
search results and find yourself another seller.

Researching the Vehicle

When you've determined that the seller is trustwor-
thy, it's time to look at the vehicle.

Getting a lemon is one of the biggest fears of buyers on eBay Motors. But there are many things you
can do to minimize the risk, and eBay puts them all
at your fingertips.

Vehicle History Reports

Many sellers offer a free CARFAX or AutoCheck report for their vehicle to show you the vehicle history and prove the title is clean. If it's not posted, e-mail the seller to ask if he or she has one. Many will provide it for you if you ask. If not, you can order one yourself.

Driver's Ed

AutoCheck is less well known than CARFAX, but it's managed by Experian (one of the major credit reporting agencies) and it has a good reputation among many dealerships as well as online sites. It's also cheaper than CARFAX.

The prices vary by which company you buy the report from, and whether you just want one report or a subscription to allow you to check multiple vehicles. AutoCheck's single report is cheaper ($7.99 versus $19.99), but CARFAX has an unlimited reports option for $24.99 a month that might be better if you're still shopping round. AutoCheck also has 10-report subscription for $14.99.

To get an AutoCheck report, click on the History Report tab in the auction listing and select the type of report you want (single or 10 report subscription). It automatically pulls the relevant information from the listing (so you have less to fill out).

To get a vehicle history report from CARFAX, copy the *VIN* from the auction listing page and go to www.carfax.com. Enter the VIN and click Search.

Follow the prompts on the screen, and you'll have the CARFAX report in less than a couple minutes.

def•i•ni•tion

VIN stands for Vehicle Identification Number and is assigned to your vehicle by the factory manufacturer. It is usually located under the hood and on the corner of the dashboard. The VIN is like your vehicle's fingerprint or Social Security number. Everything to do with its history is reported and identified using the VIN.

Independent Inspection

You can request a third-party vehicle inspection by clicking *Order an independent inspection* in the Vehicle Information section of the auction listing page.

The inspection company, SGS, performs a 150-point inspection and then puts the report online for you to see, usually within 24 hours. The service costs just under $100 for most vehicles, but if you're planning to spend $15,000, that's not very much.

Check Engine

Right next to the link to get an independent inspection, you might see the word "Inspected." This means the seller claims it has been inspected. eBay doesn't require any proof, so don't rely on this unless you get to see the inspection report.

I can't say anything about the quality of SGS inspections because I haven't personally used them, but the cost seems to be reasonable, and the turnover time is very quick. Plus, it's a third party, which makes me more comfortable with the accuracy of the report.

In my opinion, you should never buy a vehicle on eBay Motors without an inspection of some kind. When you consider the cost of most vehicles, $100 is a small price to pay for peace of mind on a purchase this big.

You must get the seller's permission before ordering through SGS because the seller must be present at the inspection. You will need to have the VIN, Make and Model, and the seller's contact information when you order the inspection.

How Much to Bid

As with any item on eBay, you should look at the off-eBay prices before making a purchase.

To research the current average selling price of the vehicle you have in mind, go to www.Edmunds.com, www.Nadaguides.com, www.KBB.com, or all three.

Most dealerships now use NADA Guides to look at used-car values, but Edmunds takes into account where you are geographically located and tells you how much people in your area are actually paying for this particular vehicle (called the True Market Value, or TMV).

Call around your local dealerships and ask for the Internet manager. Give him the specifications of the vehicle you are looking at, and ask him if he has anything similar and what out-the-door price you would be looking at. Be sure it includes any destination fee (as many dealerships add that in later).

Also ask how much the "doc fee" will be. This is a document fee that most dealers charge, and varies from state to state. When you've added it all up, this will give you an indication of your local price.

eBay Vehicle Research

Now you know what the vehicle is worth off eBay, you need to compare your research to eBay prices. Obviously, there is no point in looking at the current highest bid for ongoing auctions, because until it ends, that price can always go up. Using the *Completed Listings*, you can see exactly what vehicles are selling for on eBay.

def•i•ni•tion

> **Completed Listings** show all vehicles within your search requirements that have ended recently (usually within two weeks). If the price is in red, the vehicle did not sell. You should be looking for auctions with green prices because those items did sell.

At the top left of the auction listing page, next to the title, you'll see a link to research that make and model. For example, it might say Research Ford Mustang or Research Mazda Miata.

Clicking on this link takes you to the main category page for that make and model. You'll land on the Price Research tab, which shows you the price range of vehicles matching your make, model, and year that have sold on eBay. It also shows you the average Kelley Blue Book retail value.

Under the Just Sold heading, you can link straight to the Completed Listings page (you may have to sign into eBay again to access this page).

Watch Out for Hidden Fees

Car dealers often add "document fees" or "processing fees" or even "destination fees" to the final bid. You see this inside dealerships, too, but it's important to add it into the price when you're comparing prices from car dealers and private-party sellers (who usually don't charge these fees).

Sometimes dealers post this fee information on their About Me page and put a link in the auction to "read the terms and conditions." Be sure you do this so you know what you're agreeing to.

Sales Tax

If you purchase a vehicle in-state, you have to pay sales tax to the seller. If you purchase a vehicle from an out-of-state seller (or for some reason didn't pay the tax to an in-state seller) you are responsible for paying any taxes due when you register the vehicle in your state.

A common misconception among buyers is that buying a vehicle on the Internet is "tax free." You are required to produce a bill of sale or receipt showing what you paid for the vehicle when you register it in your state.

Different states have different rules, so be sure to talk to your Department of Motor Vehicles (DMV) before making a purchase so you don't get a nasty surprise when you register it. Your local office should be able to explain the transfer and registration process (and fees) as well. The website for each state's Department of Motor Vehicles is available in Appendix B.

If you purchase your vehicle through an out-of-state dealership, they may be required to collect some or all of the sales tax at the time of sale. This is reflected on your paperwork so when you register the vehicle in your home state, the tax is shown as completely or partially paid.

Shipping

Chapter 5 is dedicated to arranging shipping and budgeting for the cost, so I won't go into too much detail here. However, this is something you should consider before setting your maximum bid. If you are looking at local vehicles only, you can ignore shipping costs. The only cost to you is the gas each way.

Another option is flying. This is becoming more and more popular because it is often cheaper than shipping. You are also in control of the vehicle and know that it has not been damaged in transit.

The distance and the type of extra services you want (closed shipping container, top row on a car carrier, insurance, etc.) determines the price of shipping using an auto shipping company. You should expect it to be between $350 to $1,200, depending on the distance traveled. Deduct the quoted shipping cost from your maximum bid so you don't end up overpaying for the vehicle.

Budget and Bidding Wars

Bidding wars (i.e., two or more bidders going head-to-head for the same item, driving the final price up) are common on eBay.com. However, you're far less likely to get into a last-second bidding war on eBay Motors, but it's still a concern. You've spent the time to do the research properly, and you know the maximum you should pay for the vehicle. Don't go over that.

When you place your bid, eBay only shows the minimum bid. So if there is no Reserve on the auction and you bid $10,000 (when the starting price is $1,000), the bid will show up as $1,000.

Now, if any other buyer places a bid up to $10,000, they will be automatically outbid by you and the current bid will go up two more increments (one for the other buyer and then one more for you outbidding him).

If there is a Reserve on the auction (look for "Reserve not met" below the current bid), then your bid will take you straight up to the reserve price. So if the starting bid was $1,000, but the reserve price was $8,000, and you bid $10,000, the current bid would immediately jump to $8,000 and the "Reserve not met" tag would disappear. Now it will go up in the minimum increments like the no-reserve auction.

If your bid was $10,000, but the Reserve Price was $12,000, you would get a message from eBay that you are the high bidder but the reserve is not yet met. However, the current bid would display as $10,000. The seller is not obligated to sell to you even though you are the high bidder, unless your bid reaches or exceeds the reserve.

If you get outbid, it's tempting to place "one more bid," but you have no idea how high a bid that other buyer placed or how high the Reserve is set. It could be $500 higher, or it could be $5,000. If you hit your maximum bid and get outbid, walk away. It's the hardest thing to do, but otherwise you will be over-paying. Plus, you may be limited by the amount of financing you can get.

The Least You Need to Know

- Be sure your seller has a proven track record by checking their time on eBay, feedback score and rating, and the actual comments left by previous buyers (and what they bought).

- Be sure your seller has a good amount of feedback as a seller, not just as a buyer.

- Always get a vehicle history report before you bid.

- You can get an independent third-party inspection of any vehicle you are considering for about $100.

- Use other websites as well as eBay's research tools to determine your maximum bid. After you've set your maximum, stick to it.

- Watch out for hidden fees tacked on to the final bid. These can be called document fees, transaction/processing fees, or destination fees.

Signing on the Dotted Line

In This Chapter

- Making sure your money gets to the right person
- When and how to use the eBay Financing Center
- Risky payment methods to avoid
- Why sellers require a deposit and how to pay it
- Steering clear of escrow scams

You've done it! You've bought a vehicle through eBay Motors. Usually, when you buy a vehicle, you hand over a check (or sign financing documents) and drive away in your new car. The whole process takes a few hours at most. However, because most sales on eBay Motors are conducted across state lines, the payment and delivery processes are a little different.

This is probably a new experience for you, unless you've bought a preordered vehicle before. It's a strange mix between excitement of having just bought a new vehicle and apprehension about the next steps.

Right now you need to send thousands of dollars across the country before you even lay eyes on your vehicle. That's bound to cause some anxiety, but using the most secure payment method available helps alleviate some of that.

PayPal Deposits

Most vehicle sellers, particularly dealers, require a deposit (usually around $500) within 24 to 48 hours of the auction's end. On Buy It Now auctions, the deposit is usually required immediately (via PayPal).

That might seem like a lot of cash to shell out immediately, but it protects the seller from competitors just clicking Buy It Now to get rid of the competitive listings with no intention of actually buying the vehicle. And it also protects the sellers from buyers who are not serious about actually purchasing the vehicle.

Very few sellers allow total payment via PayPal—usually only sellers of low-priced vehicles, ATVs, or parts and accessories. There are two reasons: PayPal fees and transaction limits.

If you bought a set of wheel rims on eBay Motors for $1,300, the PayPal fee to the seller would be between $28.90 and $38.00, depending on his or her monthly transaction volume. That isn't too bad, and most sellers would prefer PayPal for such a transaction.

Driver's Ed

PayPal fees vary based on the total payments the seller receives each month. Most people are charged 2.9 percent of the payment amount plus $0.30. However, if the seller's volume is higher than $3,000 per month, he or she pays a lower percentage.

Now let's say you paid the seller $10,000 for a vehicle. Now the PayPal fee is $220. This is more than most sellers want to lose from profit when there are alternative payment options.

So most sellers require a $500 deposit via PayPal (fee to them is between $11.30 and $14.80) and then the rest of the payment via a method that doesn't cost the seller any further fees.

Incidentally, there's a reason I picked $10,000 for my example. This is the maximum payment PayPal allows. So your total (including shipping) must be below that amount. You lose all fraud protection if you send multiple payments to get around this transaction limit, so don't even consider it.

Because you can't use PayPal for the entire purchase, it's now time to look at what you can use.

eBay Financing Center

However much I would love to take a suitcase of cash to a dealership and buy my dream car on the spot, it just isn't going to happen. In fact, very few people buying a vehicle have cash in the bank to pay for it outright. Most of us take out a loan to cover at least part of the cost.

eBay helps you find a lender through the eBay Financing Center. You can link there using the Get Low Monthly Payments link below the current bid on most auction pages. Alternatively, you can go directly to financing-center.ebay.com.

Driver's Ed

In the eBay Financing Centers, you'll also find a tool to estimate your monthly payment and a link to the Auto Insurance Center to research insurance rates for your new vehicle.

eBay matches you with a lender based on the type of vehicle you are purchasing, the manufacturer of the vehicle, the amount you need to borrow, and which state you are in. The main lenders are HSBC Auto Finance, Capital One Auto Finance, and E-Loan. You can find financing for pretty much any vehicle for sale on eBay through the Financing Center.

You're not really going to save much time by using the eBay Financing Center because you still have to physically sign and return paperwork and the loan check will be mailed to you.

You can get overnight service for a fee (usually $15), which expedites the process, but because you can walk out of your bank with a check in hand, it's not really saving you time by beginning the process online.

There are, however, three important things that make the loans through the eBay Financing Center a little easier than through other lenders:

1. They are all approved for out-of-state purchases.

2. Purchases can be made from either a dealer or private seller.

3. None of them require an inspection by the lender prior to loan approval.

If you're not using the eBay Financing Center to get your loan, you need to be sure your lender accepts all three of those conditions for the loan before you place a bid.

Check Engine

I strongly advise you get your loan pre-approved before you bid. Remember, bidding on an eBay auction is a legally binding contract. If you win an auction, you are legally obligated to purchase the item, whether it is a $20 Beatles album or a $20,000 Volkswagen Beetle. Don't bid before you know you can pay. Not being able to get financing after the auction ends is not an excuse for backing out of a winning bid.

Look at all your financing options. Just because eBay endorses certain companies doesn't mean they are the right lenders for you. You might find a cheaper rate or better terms at your regular bank or a local credit union, so it's worth shopping around.

Other Payment Options

If you end up financing through your own bank, you may find you get the funds deposited into your checking account. Most sellers do not accept personal checks because the funds are not guaranteed until the check clears. However, there are a number of other options.

Escrow

There are four steps to paying for an online purchase using escrow:

1. The buyer sends the full payment to the escrow company.
2. The seller verifies that the funds are available and sends the item to the buyer.
3. The buyer receives the item in the condition agreed and releases the funds to the seller.
4. The seller receives the payment for the item.

The escrow company keeps the funds in a non–interest bearing account until the buyer instructs them to release it.

Escrow is the most secure payment transfer method and the only one that lets you inspect the vehicle prior to paying the seller. However, it isn't free. The company charges a fee for their service, and it is usually paid for by the person who requests the service. However, many sellers will split the cost with you.

Escrow.com Fees as of November 2007

Vehicle Price	Escrow.com Fee
Up to $7,500	$125
$7,500.01–$15,000	$170
$15,000.01–$30,000	$200
$30,000.01–$50,000	$275
Over $50,000	0.6% of vehicle price

The only escrow company recommended by eBay is www.escrow.com.

Beware of Fake Escrow Websites

Getting taken in by one of the fake website or fake escrow company scams is a scary situation, considering the amount of money changing hands. This is how the scam goes:

1. You win an auction for a car.

2. You get an e-mail from the seller saying he wants to use an escrow company and will pay for it, and gives you a link to go to the site. The problem is, the link takes you to a fake site. It may look like a legitimate escrow company site (or even a copy of escrow.com), but it isn't.

3. You follow all the registration steps, giving the scammer your personal and banking information, and arrange for the transfer of funds to the company.

4. You never receive the car, or the money. The seller cancels his eBay account and is never heard from again.

This is why researching the seller is so important. It's okay to buy from a relatively new seller, but I never buy from someone with zero feedback or who has only registered on eBay in the last 30 days.

The escrow scam is easily avoided. First, never click on an e-mail link that is supposed to take you to an escrow company (even escrow.com). Secondly, always insist on using escrow.com rather than another service that you may have never heard of. The website may be legitimate, but sometimes the company itself isn't.

Escrow is one of the securest methods of paying for a high-priced item (whether it's an expensive piece of artwork or a Porsche Boxster) and is probably your best option if you're okay with shelling out the cash for it.

Bank Wire Transfer

Transferring funds directly from one bank to another is a good way of tracking a payment and ensuring funds are immediately available. There is no question about whether the seller received it or not because there is a direct paper trail from your account to hers.

However, most sellers don't want to give out their personal banking information. She would have to give you her bank account number and routing number to set up the transfer. So you would have her full name, address, and banking details. In the wrong hands, that could be dangerous.

If you are planning to use a bank wire transfer, be sure to request the seller's information through eBay and ensure the name and address match what the seller gave you for the transfer destination. If not, don't do it.

To get a seller's contact information:

1. Click Advanced Search by the main search box on any eBay Motors page.
2. Click Find Contact Information in the bottom left box.
3. Enter the seller's User ID and the transaction number for the closed auction.
4. eBay will e-mail you and the seller with the other person's registered contact information, including telephone numbers.

As you may have gathered, I'm not really a fan of bank transfers. I think there are better options that are safer for all parties. Still, they are far safer than instant money transfer services like MoneyGram or Western Union (I talk about those in a few moments). If you and the seller happen to bank at the same place, then your risk is significantly reduced, but you won't know that until you get the seller's banking information.

Cashier's Check

Most people consider a cashier's check like cash. It's not. It's simply a check that cannot bounce because the funds in your bank account are put on hold as soon as the check is issued. It is still subject to clearing times and, therefore, open to check fraud.

There are some scams that target buyers and some that attack sellers. The cashier's check scam is one that goes after sellers, so most sellers are cautious when dealing with cashier's checks.

There is a popular myth that checks clear in two days. The truth is that the funds *become available* in two days, but the check may not clear the issuing bank for two weeks. If it turns out that it is a fake, it may not be caught until the check is returned by the issuing bank. If the seller has already shipped the vehicle and transferred the title, he's now got a lot of problems.

Because of this, most sellers put a hold on the check until it clears their bank. Many banks put a hold on checks (even cashier's checks) over $5,000, so the seller may have no choice in the matter.

If you are paying a seller in person, this is the method I recommend. Most sellers won't put a hold on a local cashier's check because he or she can go to the issuing bank and receive cash immediately without the check having to go through the clear-inghouse system.

If you do send a cashier's check to a seller by mail, be sure it is sent via a courier service that requires a signature and offers tracking services (such as UPS, FedEx, DHL, etc.). If it is lost, your issuing branch can cancel and then reissue it, but that's more hassle than you need. If a problem arises, cashier's checks can be traced to the receiving account in the same way as any other check, so from a buyer's perspective, it's not a bad option.

Cash

If you're lucky enough to have enough money in your bank account to cover the cost of your purchase, you might be tempted to show up with the suitcase of cash that I mentioned earlier. As fun as this sounds, there are a lot of risks involved. First, you can't trace the money once it has been handed over. How can you prove exactly how much you paid, or that you did in fact pay anything? Second, walking around with that much money is just asking to be mugged.

I really don't advise using cash unless it's a relatively inexpensive item (under $1,500). Most sellers don't want to receive a lot in cash anyway.

If you do pay in cash, don't be surprised or offended if the seller has a counterfeit detection pen or light. If you deposit that much cash into your bank, they will check it the same way. After the seller signs over the title to you, he's got no recourse if the money turns out to be counterfeit, so he's just protecting himself.

One last thing—unless you like throwing money away, don't ever mail cash.

Unsafe Payment Methods to Avoid

As far as deposit payments are concerned, be sure you check eBay's list of "accepted" and "not accepted" online payment services before you send a payment. You can access the full policy at pages.ebay.com/help/policies/accepted-payments-policy.html and then click on Some Examples to view the two lists. I always use PayPal or BidPay and recommend you do the same, but some sellers prefer other online payment services. So long as they are on the accepted list, you should be fine.

Instant Cash Transfers

Western Union, MoneyGram, and other such services are great when you're sending cash to your kids in college, but they are not designed for eBay purchases, or any other transfer of funds to a stranger.

You will see warnings all over eBay Motors reminding you not to use Western Union or MoneyGram. This is not eBay slamming PayPal's competitors; it is an important warning because neither service is secure for payments to strangers. Here's why:

- You can't trace an instant cash transfer.
- It is impossible to guarantee who received the funds.
- You can't cancel an instant cash transfer.
- Recovering funds in the event of fraud is very difficult.

In fact, both Western Union and MoneyGram have letters posted on eBay's website specifically telling users not to use their services for eBay purchases. If you're interested, you can read them at pages.ebay.com/securitycenter/mrkt_safety/instantcashtransfer.html. The bottom line is, they are great when you know the recipient personally, but not safe if you don't.

The Least You Need to Know

- Get preapproved for your loan before you place a bid.
- Never use Western Union or MoneyGram for any eBay purchase.
- Escrow is the only payment method that allows you to inspect the vehicle prior to releasing funds.
- If you want to use an escrow company, insist on escrow.com, and never click an e-mail link to any escrow company website.
- Don't be surprised if your seller puts a hold time on your cashier's check.

How Do I Get My Vehicle?

In This Chapter

- Questions to ask when you get a shipping quote
- How to compare quotes from multiple companies
- Researching the shipping company

If you buy a vehicle locally, you'll just pick it up from the seller. If you're within a day's drive, it might be worth costing out the fly and drive option (i.e., fly to pick up the vehicle and drive it home). If the vehicle is large, heavy, or modified, this may well be the cheapest option for you.

Click on the Shipping tab on the auction listing page and scroll to the bottom of the page. From here you can search for flights to the nearest airport (it works out the closest one for you).

Also on the Shipping tab you will see three quotes for vehicle shipping from eBay's preferred partners: Express Auto Transport, United Road, and Dependable Auto Shippers (DAS).

Finding the Right Auto Carrier for You

When deciding on a vehicle shipper, it's important
to do your research. Of the three shippers eBay
recommends, only Express Auto Transport is a
member of the Better Business Bureau. Still, there
are other ways to find out about carriers.

At www.transportreviews.com, you can find listings
for hundreds of carriers where previous customers
can post reviews about their service, delivery, any
problems, etc. Some carriers post responses, so you
get both sides of the issue. As with most review
sites, you will see the really good and really bad
reviews and not much in the middle. Still, it's worth
looking through.

All Shipping Quotes Are Not Created Equal

On the eBay Shipping tab, you will see a quote
from each of the preferred partners. However, not
all quotes cover the same things. I contacted each of
the shipping companies directly so I could compare
their quotes side by side. The vehicle quoted was
a 2004 Honda Accord to be shipped from Dallas,
Texas (75201), to Seattle, Washington (98101).

Quote Comparison of eBay Preferred Shipping Companies

Shipper	Door-to-Door	Terminal-to-Terminal	Insurance Cost	Deductible
Express Auto Transport	$935	N/A	Included	None
United Road	$1,200	$1,140	Included	None
Dependable Auto Shippers	$883	$677	$179	$250

Quotes are for the eBay Motors rate for a shipment on November 21, 2007.

You have to be careful when getting online quotes because some companies just show you the cheapest quote and then add on all the extras later. Be sure when you compare quotes they are for the same services (i.e., door-to-door, including insurance, deductible cost, etc.).

Plus, remember you can only do terminal-to-terminal shipping if the seller will deliver it to the originating terminal. You may have to pay him or her extra to do that. Also be sure you have a terminal near you before making a final decision. The nearest terminal on your end may be several hours away.

Insurance

After your vehicle is picked up, it's completely in the carrier's hands. With this in mind, you absolutely have to have insurance. As soon as you purchase the vehicle, get it added to your own auto policy. Explain to your insurance agent how it is being shipped and confirm that you are covered and how much your deductible will be if there is any damage.

If the auto shipper has insurance, be sure you get information about the limits, coverage, etc. You also need to find out the deductible (if any). Both Express Auto Transport and United Road include the premium in the original quote price, and neither charge a deductible. DAS keeps both separate. They call it "valuation."

If you have good auto insurance coverage, and a low deductible for both comprehensive and collision, it's probably worth considering using your own insurance if you have the choice. In the case of DAS, the insurance premium is $179, plus $250 for the deductible if they damage the vehicle. So you could get a cheaper quote if you don't need the insurance. But don't do it if your auto deductible would be higher than the insurance premium and deductible from the carrier.

Even if your chosen carrier has excellent insurance, it pays to have your own policy as backup. So be sure to add the new vehicle to your insurance as soon as it is paid for.

How to Compare Quotes

When you get a quote for shipping (either online or via phone) be sure you know exactly what is covered. Look at the total cost including insurance when you're comparing quotes.

When you call, be sure to ask for eBay Motors discounts, or any other discounts that may apply. If you are in the military or belong to an organization that often gets discounts (AAA, AARP, etc.), ask for that discount, as it may be better than the eBay Motors discount rate. The worst they can say is no.

Be sure the quote is for the exact vehicle you are shipping. A quote for one vehicle is not necessarily going to be the same rate as for another vehicle, even if it's coming from the same place. Factors that affect the rate include the following:

- Type of vehicle (car, truck, SUV)
- Modifications to vehicle
- Whether it runs or not
- Closed carrier required (usually used for classic cars)
- Guaranteed top level (so no fluids from other vehicles can drip on it)
- How quickly you need to have the vehicle picked up
- If you need a guaranteed date and time for pick up versus a date range
- Convertible top

I highly recommend you call and talk with a representative. The phone numbers and website addresses for each of the eBay preferred shipping companies are available in Appendix B.

When you do ship a vehicle, keep your quote number, tracking number, order paperwork, extension number of the ordering agent, and everything else that pertains to the shipment. Ask the seller to fax or mail you the carrier's inspection sheet where they noted all existing damage before they took possession of the vehicle. If you don't have this, you have no reference point for when you receive the vehicle and do the post-shipment inspection.

The Least You Need to Know

- It may be cheaper and less hassle to fly to where your new vehicle is located and drive it home.

- Go to www.transportreviews.com to see reviews from actual customers of the various shipping companies.

- Always be sure you have added the vehicle to your insurance policy before having it shipped.

- When comparing shipping quotes, be sure you have the same options on all of them.

- Always ask for discounts. They are not going to volunteer them unless you ask.

- Keep all paperwork together and easy to find. You might just need it.

Chapter 6

What If Something Goes Wrong?

In This Chapter

- What to do if you accidentally placed the wrong bid
- Restrictions for bid retractions
- Fraud protection for vehicle buyers
- Fraud protection for parts and accessories buyers

If you've followed the steps in this book and kept a close watch for red flags, you shouldn't have any trouble completing your transaction. However, sometimes things do go wrong.

In this chapter, we look at what happens if you are unfortunate enough to have a problem with your transaction, and what you can do about it.

When You Can and Can't Retract Your Bid

eBay understands that everyone makes mistakes. If you accidently bid $10,000 instead of $1,000, don't panic. You can retract your bid, so long as you immediately bid the correct amount.

There are a couple other instances when it is okay to retract a bid:

- If the seller makes changes to the description that significantly alters the item you are bidding on (he said the part fit model years 2000–2006 but then later corrected it to 2004–2006 and you have a 2002 model).

- You cannot reach the seller (this means you've tried his phone number and the number is a nonworking number, or the e-mails you sent are returned as undeliverable).

Check Engine

You cannot retract your bid if you used the Buy It Now option on an auction or fixed price listing. Once you confirm the purchase, you are obligated to pay for it.

Here are some reasons I've heard for wanting to retract a bid that are not allowed:

- You decide you didn't really want to bid that high, or decide you don't want the item at all.

- You didn't get financing arranged before bidding, and it turns out you can't finance the amount you bid.

- Your kid, dog, cat, gecko, etc. got on your computer and bid without you realizing it.

This last example is a lame excuse and one I've heard way too many times. You have to confirm the bid after you enter it, so unless your cat is particularly handy with the mouse (pardon the pun), this really isn't likely to happen.

You are responsible for bids placed through your account, whether it's by your spouse, teenager, or even pet. If you're concerned about this, always log out before leaving the computer. I doubt very much that your cat can type your password as well.

If you do find yourself in one of these situations, you can contact the seller and request they cancel the bid for you. Most of the time they will because they want to be sure the winning bidder is going to pay. Still, they are not obligated to do it.

How to Retract a Bid

There is a simple form to complete. You'll need the item number, so copy that to your clipboard (or write it down) before going to the form. For a regular auction bid retraction, go to offer.ebay. com/ws/eBayISAPI.dll?RetractBidShow. Or go to the Site Map and click Bid Retractions under the Buying Resources heading.

If you need to retract a Best Offer go to offer.ebay.
com/ws/eBayISAPI.dll?RetractBestOfferShow.

Timing Restrictions on Bid Retractions

If you placed your bid *more than 12 hours* from the end
of the auction, you can retract your bid up until those
last 12 hours begin. So if the auction ends at 8:00 P.M.
on Tuesday, you would have to retract your bid before
8:00 A.M. on Tuesday morning. If you ask nicely, a
seller can cancel your bid within the last 12 hours, but
he is not obligated to do so.

If you placed a bid *during the last 12 hours* of the
auction, you can retract it up to 1 hour after it was
placed without the seller's permission. So if the auction ends at 8:00 P.M. and you placed your bid at
1:00 P.M., you have until 2:00 P.M. to retract that
bid. If it's later than that, you'll have to ask the
seller to cancel your bid (but he is not required to
do so).

For more information about bid retraction, go
to pages.ebay.com/help/buy/questions/retract-bid.
html.

Fraud Protection from eBay— Exclusive for eBay Motors

Fraud is a concern whenever you make an Internet
purchase. Unless you're an antiques collector, a
vehicle is probably the highest-priced item you
would buy through eBay. Because of this, eBay has
some additional fraud protection for eBay Motors.

The fraud-protection services on eBay Motors come under the Vehicle Protection Program. The two main elements to this are Vehicle Purchase Protection and Condition Guarantee by Seller.

Vehicle Purchase Protection (VPP)

This is the main fraud protection you get for buying a vehicle on eBay Motors. The eligibility and coverage depends on the type of vehicle you purchased, so these are just some of the main highlights. To learn all about Vehicle Purchase Protection go to pages.motors.ebay. com/buy/purchase-protection/index.html or click the Vehicle Purchase Protection link on the eBay Motors homepage.

There are two main types of protection covered by VPP …

1. Gross material misrepresentation protection:

- Undisclosed damage to the vehicle
- Misrepresented vehicle year/make/model
- Misrepresented odometer reading
- Undisclosed salvage title

2. Fraud protection:

- Vehicle not received
- Vehicle received is a stolen vehicle
- Vehicle received has an undisclosed lien on it
- Vehicle received without a title (only if both buyer's and seller's state departments require a title certificate for the vehicle)

Coverage amounts:

- Up to $20,000 or the total vehicle price plus up to $800 in transportation costs, whichever is lower.

- You pay a $100 processing fee when your claim is finalized (paid out of the amount you will receive).

- There are minimum damage requirements for material misrepresentation claims, so be sure to look at them at pages.motors.ebay.com/services/purchase-protection.html.

Eligibility:

- Legal purchase of a motorcycle, ATV, go-kart, scooter, moped, personal watercraft, snowmobile, boat, RV, commercial truck, bus, race car, trailer (non-RV), camper, car, or truck.

- Vehicle must be listed in one of these five categories: Cars and Trucks, Motorcycles, Powersports, Boats, or Other Vehicles and Trailers.

- Payment must be sent to a U.S. bank, and the vehicle, buyer, and seller must all be in the United States at the time of the transaction (includes Alaska and Hawaii).

- Purchase must be made on eBay Motors, and the buyer must be identified as the winning bidder/buyer on the closed listing page. Purchasing a vehicle directly from the seller (i.e., off eBay) voids this protection.

- The feedback rating for both buyer and seller must be zero or higher (i.e., not –1, –2, etc.).

- A buyer may only file one claim per six months for a car/truck purchase, or twice every six months for other vehicles.

- The buyer must wait 14 days before initiating the claim and must have already attempted to work out the issue with the seller (proof will be required).

- If the purchase was made with a credit card, the buyer must file a claim with the credit card company first. Proof of a denied claim will be required.

- A claim through the Vehicle Purchase Protection must be filed within 35 days of the end of listing. If a title is missing or you discover an undisclosed lien, you have 90 days to file the claim. If you discover the vehicle was previously stolen, you have six months to file the claim.

These are just general highlights. Each type of vehicle has specific requirements for eligibility, which you can link to by clicking Eligibility on the Vehicle Purchase Protection page or going directly to pages.motors.ebay.com/buy/purchase-protection/eligibility.html.

Condition Guarantee by Seller

Whereas the Vehicle Purchase Protection covers all of the major issues of fraud and misrepresentation, Condition Guarantee by Seller covers minor discrepancies from the item description. There is a $250 deductible, and this coverage only applies to passenger vehicles that are 8 years old or younger. This is not an automatic coverage; the seller must be enrolled in this program for you to be covered. The program is limited to dealers who are also large volume sellers.

Driver's Ed

The purpose of Condition Guarantee by Seller is similar to the PowerSeller program. These are trusted sellers who have proven themselves in the eBay Motors marketplace. They should work with you if there is an issue, so only if they cannot solve the problem satisfactorily should you be using the eBay Motors claims process.

Sellers who are part of the Condition Guarantee by Seller program are guaranteeing that the vehicle condition is as described, and that they will work with you to ensure your satisfaction.

Condition Guarantee By Seller does not cover the following:

- High-line exotic vehicles (Alfa Romeo, Aston Martin, Lamborghini, Lotus, Hummer, Ferrari, etc.)
- Modified vehicles or "kit" cars
- Vehicles with an "other" title or a title marked as salvage, rebuilt/rebuildable,

> unrebuildable, scrapped/destroyed, junk, lemon, or water damaged

- Vehicles with more than 125,000 miles

The minimum claim is $500, and the maximum coverage is $10,000 or 50 percent of the vehicle cost, whichever is lower. Don't forget there is a $250 deductible on all claims, too.

There are a lot of specifics for what is and what is not covered by this service. Rather than taking pages to list them, you can view them at pages. motors.ebay.com/services/conditionguarantee.html.

Look for the Condition Guarantee by Seller seal to see if an item is eligible for coverage.

Condition Guarantee by Seller Seal.

You are still covered for the fraud portion of the Vehicle Purchase Protection even if you file a claim through Condition Guaranteed by Seller.

PayPal Buyer Protection

If you're purchasing parts or accessories, you are not covered by Vehicle Purchase Protection; however, you may be covered by PayPal Buyer Protection. This is the general fraud protection for the main eBay site. It requires you to pay via

PayPal but will cover you up to $200 without a processing fee. If the seller qualifies, you could be covered up to $2,000. The seller requirements for the top-tier coverage are:

- Feedback score of 50 or more.
- 98 percent positive feedback rating.
- Seller has a verified premier or verified business PayPal account.
- Listing must be on eligible eBay site.
- The seller is a PayPal user from one of 38 eligible countries.
- PayPal must be a listed payment option on the auction.

On the auction listing page, in the Buy Safely box (right-hand side underneath the Meet the Seller box), you'll see a line that tells you how much the item is covered for. If the seller qualifies for the top-tier coverage, it will say "This item is covered up to $2,000. See eligibility." You can see all the terms and conditions by clicking "See eligibility."

As well as seller requirements, there are certain things you need to do to qualify for PayPal Buyer Protection:

- You bought the item on eBay (you must show up on eBay's site as the winning bidder to be covered).
- You paid the seller using the Pay Now button on the closed auction page, in My eBay, or in the winning bidder e-mail eBay sent

you. Alternatively, you can manually enter the item number when you send the PayPal payment.

- You must have a PayPal account. If you used your credit card through PayPal without actually having an account, you will have to sign up before you can file a claim based on that transaction.

- You paid for the item in one payment (i.e., not split up) to the registered PayPal address provided by eBay Checkout. Even if the seller asks you to use a different address, don't because you would then be ineligible for coverage.

- You filed the claim within 45 days of when you originally sent the payment. You have 20 days from when you first filed a dispute to escalate it to a claim.

It may seem like there are a lot of requirements and exclusions, and there are. This protection is like an insurance policy, PayPal (and eBay) have to look at the risk assessment for offering this coverage. If they gave a blanket coverage for all transactions and all sellers, the number of claims would skyrocket, which is not cost-effective for eBay.

You should rely on your research to find a good seller and item. Do everything you can to be sure this is an above-board transaction, and then if something does end up going wrong, you know you did all you could and you can then fall back on the fraud-protection coverage.

The Least You Need to Know

- Most vehicle sales on eBay Motors are covered by the Vehicle Purchase Protection Program for up to $20,000.

- Look for the Condition Guarantee by Seller seal on the auction page to see if the item qualifies for this fraud protection.

- Condition Guarantee by Seller gives you extra protection when you're buying a passenger vehicle from a trusted seller.

- Parts and accessories purchases are covered by eBay's regular fraud protection, PayPal Buyer Protection, provided the buyer uses PayPal for the full payment.

- Be sure you follow the requirements for the fraud-protection programs, or you might find yourself ineligible for coverage.

eBay Motors for Sellers

Whether you're looking to sell your car, ATV, boat, or parts and accessories, eBay Motors helps you market your items to millions of potential buyers. Why rely on local newspapers and classifieds sites when you can reach a much wider audience without a lot of extra effort?

This part shows you how to sell, what price to expect, how to deal with receiving payments, and how to protect yourself from fraud. There is a steep learning curve to selling on eBay Motors. We start with the basics and follow every step of the selling process. By the end of this part, you'll be a confident eBay Motors seller and understand all the main aspects of selling, whether you're a private-party seller or a dealer.

What You Should Know Before Selling on eBay Motors

In This Chapter

- How to become a registered seller
- Getting PayPal Verified and confirming your address
- Removing withdrawal limits
- Feedback from a seller's point of view
- How to get good feedback

Before you sell, I strongly recommend you get some experience buying. If you're a vehicle dealer, it is tempting to jump in and start selling like you do on your own website. However, building some feedback, and learning how eBay differs from other websites, are important steps in your journey to success as an eBay Motors seller.

Before you start selling, you must take certain steps to become fully registered and ready to sell.

Registering as a Seller in Five Easy Steps

This is really simple, particularly if you've already put your credit card on file to become a verified buyer (as I discussed in Chapter 1). You'll need a check and your credit or debit card (MasterCard, Visa, American Express, or Discover), so get those now before you start the process.

1. Click the Sell tab on the top navigation bar and select Sell Your Item.

2. Click Create Seller's Account.

3. Complete the credit card information and click Continue. If you already added the information when you became a verified buyer, you will see the last four digits of the card already filled in. You will need to add the card verification number again, but that's it.

4. Enter your checking account information using the information on your check and click Continue.

5. Now you need to choose how to pay your selling fees. These are debited automatically each month if you owe anything. You can make a payment through My eBay at any time if you want to use a method other than your default. Your choice for the default method is using either your credit card or checking account. I don't really see any benefit of one over the other, so just choose whichever is most convenient for you and then click Continue.

That's it; you're now registered as a seller. The page you're on now is the beginning of the Sell Your Item form. From now on, if you click the Sell tab on the navigation bar, this is where it takes you.

If you don't have a credit or debit card, you can still become a seller by completing the ID Verify program (as explained in Chapter 1). It costs $5, but if you don't have a credit or debit card and want to sell, you don't really have any other option.

PayPal for Sellers

If you haven't already done this, go to www.paypal.com and register. You need to be sure you have both your credit card and bank account on file with PayPal, too (eBay and PayPal don't share this information), so that you will have both a *Confirmed Address* and be *PayPal Verified*.

Most buyers won't buy from a unverified seller, particularly on eBay Motors, so this is an important step.

def•i•ni•tion

Having a **Confirmed Address** means you've added a credit card to your account. PayPal confirms that the credit card billing address matches the information you registered with. **PayPal Verified** means you have added a bank account and PayPal has verified that you are the owner (by depositing two small amounts that you had to confirm).

Removing Withdrawal Limits

You are restricted to withdrawing a maximum of
$500 a month from your bank account until you
remove the withdrawal limits. To do this, you can
either add your Social Security number to your
PayPal account, or complete the Expanded Use
Program.

Either way, the process begins the same.

1. Log in to PayPal.
2. Click View Limits on your My Account page
   (next to your account balance).
3. Scroll down to Withdrawal Limit and click
   the link in the sentence "Complete two of
   these three steps."

You've already completed one, by adding your bank
account. Now you need to select which of the other
two options you will choose. I never give out my
Social Security number if there is another option,
so my preference is the Expanded Use Program.
However, this can take a few days to complete and
involves charging your credit card a small amount,
so if time is of the essence, you might have to go
the Social Security number route.

To add your Social Security number, click the cor-
responding box and then enter the number on the
next page. Click Submit, and you're done. The
withdrawal limit is immediately removed, and
you're ready to go.

If you prefer to use the Expanded Use Program, then check that box instead. As I said, this takes a little extra time.

1. First, you authorize PayPal to charge your credit card $1.95 by clicking Get Number. You will be refunded the charge after your next PayPal payment.

2. When you see the charge show up on your credit card statement, look for a four-digit number next to it. This is your Expanded Use Number. Write it down and log back into PayPal.

3. On your account page, you'll see a Complete Expanded Use Program link. Click this and enter the four-digit code.

4. Your withdrawal limit will be immediately lifted.

You're going to need to upgrade your account pretty soon, too. Once you hit $500 a month in payments coming in, or five credit card transactions within a 12-month period, you have to upgrade to a Premier account. This is basically the PayPal seller's account.

Because the items you're going to be selling are higher priced than most on eBay, you will likely hit these limits quickly. The downside is that once you upgrade your account, you are charged a fee for every payment you receive from then on. Until you upgrade, you are only charged for the credit card transactions (but until you upgrade it is a much higher rate, 4.9 percent plus $0.30).

The fees are based on your monthly transaction volume.

PayPal Fees for Premier and Business Accounts

Tier	Monthly Payments Received	PayPal Fee
1	$0.00–$3,000.00	2.9% plus $0.30
2	$3,000.01–$10,000.00	2.5% plus $0.30
3	$10,000.01–$100,000.00	2.2% plus $0.30
4	Over $100,000.00	1.9% plus $0.30

Most sellers are in the first or second fee tiers because you're only receiving deposit payments or parts and accessories payments through PayPal. Here are some examples of the PayPal fees for different transaction amounts (the maximum amount allowed in a single transaction is $10,000).

PayPal Fees for Various Transaction Amounts

Transaction	Tier 1 Fee (2.9% + $0.30)	Tier 2 Fee (2.5% + $0.30)
$500	$14.80	$12.80
$1,000	$29.30	$25.30
$2,500	$72.80	$62.80
$5,000	$145.30	$125.30
$7,500	$217.80	$187.80
$10,000	$290.30	$250.30

Be sure to calculate your expected PayPal fees before you list your item. You cannot say "buyer pays PayPal fees," as this is against the terms and conditions of your PayPal account. However, you can factor them into your starting or reserve price. For a great free PayPal fee calculator, go to www.PPCalc.com.

What Does It Cost to Sell on eBay Motors?

Vehicles are treated differently from other eBay items and as such, have a different fee schedule. There are some exceptions; for example, items listed in the Powersports Vehicles Under 50cc or Motorcycles categories have different fees from the rest of eBay Motors. I'm going to break it down and make it as clear as possible, but you can also see this information on eBay at pages.ebay.com/help/sell/motorfees.html.

Insertion and Transaction Fees

You pay an Insertion fee each time you list an item on eBay. The Transaction fee (which is called the Final Value Fee for all non-eBay Motors auctions) is only paid if the listing ends in a successful sale. So if the bidding doesn't meet your reserve price, or the listing doesn't end with Buy It Now or accepted Best Offer, you do not pay a Transaction fee. If you send a Second Chance Offer to a nonwinning bidder and they accept it, then you pay the Transaction fee for that listing.

Insertion and Transaction Fees for eBay Motors

Category Item Is Listed In	Insertion Fee	Transaction Fee
Passenger Vehicles	$40.00	$50.00
Motorcycles	$30.00	$40.00
Powersports	$30.00	$40.00
Powersports Vehicles Under 50cc	$3.00	$3.00
Other Vehicles	$40.00	$50.00

All parts and accessories fees are covered in Chapter 13.

Reserve Price Auctions

In the buying chapters I mentioned Reserve Price auctions. As a seller, this allows you to set a price (higher than your starting price) that is the minimum you will sell the item for. So you can set the starting price at $2,000 to get bidding interest, but set the reserve at $20,000 if you want. Unless the bidding reaches $20,000, you are not obligated to sell to the highest bidder.

If you have a lien on your vehicle, you must set a Reserve Price—otherwise, you could end up legally bound to sell the vehicle for less than you owe on it.

There is a fee for setting a Reserve Price, but it is refunded if the item sells. I would estimate about 80 percent of eBay Motors vehicle auctions use a Reserve Price.

Reserve Price Fee for All Vehicles (Except Powersports Under 50cc)

Reserve Price	Fee
$0.01–$5,000.00	$5.00
$5,000.01–$10,000.00	0.1% of reserve price
$10,000.01 and up	$10.00

For Powersports Vehicles Under 50cc, the fee is a flat-rate $2.00.

Listing Upgrade Fees

In addition to the Insertion fee, some sellers choose to pay for upgrades to their listing to make it stand out more. I talk about each of them, and which are most useful, in Chapter 11.

eBay Motors Vehicle Listing Upgrade Fees (Excluding Powersports Under 50cc)

Listing Upgrade	Fee
Bold	$4.00
Border	$4.00
Highlight	$5.00
Listing Designer	$5.00
Gallery	Free
Gallery Plus	$2.00
Buy It Now	$1.00
Scheduled Listing	$1.00

continues

eBay Motors Vehicle Listing Upgrade Fees (Excluding Powersports Under 50cc) (continued)

Listing Upgrade	Fee
10-Day Duration	$8.00
21-Day Duration	$25.00
Featured Plus!	$19.95
Motors Home Page Featured	$99.95
Motors Pro Pack (Bold, Border, Highlight, & Featured Plus)	$29.95

Powersports Under 50cc Listing Upgrade Fees

Listing Upgrade	Fee
Bold	$1.00
Border	$3.00
Highlight	$5.00
Listing Designer	$5.00
Gallery	Free
Buy It Now	$0.05
Scheduled Listing	$0.10
10-Day Duration	$0.20
21-Day Duration	$25.00
Featured Plus!	$19.95
Motors Home Page Featured	$24.95

eBay Motors Picture Services Fees

In Chapter 9, we look at how to take good pictures for your auction. eBay wants you to include lots of photos because that's what gets buyers bidding, so they have a special deal for eBay Motors sellers. If you pay per picture, the first is free and then you pay an additional $0.15 per picture after that. But other options can be more affordable.

Picture Services Fees

Option	Fee
Supersize Pictures	$0.75
Picture Show	$1.00
Vehicle Picture Pack (24 Supersize photos)	$2.00
Powersports Vehicles Under 50cc Picture Pack (24 Supersize photos)	$2.00
Parts and Accessories Picture Pack (12 Supersize photos)	$1.00

The picture packs are cheaper if you have nine or more pictures to include.

eBay Motors sellers automatically get Gallery included as part of their Insertion fee. This places a thumbnail image next to the listing title on the results page. Non-eBay Motors listings (including Parts and Accessories) are charged $0.35 for this option.

Building Feedback

If you're a savvy buyer, you already know that buyers look for good feedback, and lots of it.

If you have a private-party vehicle to sell and have no experience on eBay yet, you are really going to need to sell some other items first. I know this sounds like more work you don't want to do, but it could translate into hundreds or possibly thousands of dollars more in bids for your vehicle, so it's worth the effort.

First, you need to buy a couple things on eBay so you have some feedback before you list your first item. These can be cheap items. There's so much on eBay, you won't have any trouble finding something you were going to buy anyway (and it will probably be a much lower price).

When you get ready to sell, sell items you have at home that you no longer need. If it's related to cars, even better. Remember that the titles of the items you sell will be on display in your feedback profile, so the more relevant they are to eBay Motors, the better.

Driver's Ed

Buyers are more likely to take a chance on a new seller if the price tag is relatively low. Savvy buyers won't even consider a new seller for a high-ticket item like a car.

If you're a car dealer, you have plenty of inventory in your parts department, and with the accessories from each manufacturer. Ball caps, key chains, etc. are great starting out items because they are inexpensive for the buyers. Price them low, so you easily get the sales. The point of this exercise is not to make money on these items; it's to start building your feedback score.

While you're starting out, it's critical that you follow the "best selling practices" so you receive good feedback from your buyers. The last thing you need right now is a negative feedback, or even a neutral. So always follow these tips:

- Price competitively so the buyer gets a good deal.

- Describe the item honestly and fully. Point out any flaws so the buyer knows exactly what he or she is buying.

- Do not overcharge for shipping.

- Pack the item *carefully* so it is protected during shipping.

- Include a thank you note inside the package.

- Use a fast shipping service. I like Priority Mail because it's cheaper than a courier, but still pretty fast.

- Respond to questions from buyers quickly, politely, and thoroughly. You're selling yourself as much as your items.

- Follow up with the buyer after the item has arrived, and always leave positive feedback before expecting the buyer to reciprocate.

If you follow these steps, you should get glowing feedback.

Detailed Seller Ratings

You won't see the Detailed Seller Ratings until you have 10 responses because eBay doesn't want sellers to be able to identify which buyers left which ratings. But when you hit 10, all of them show up at once.

Because Detailed Seller Ratings are optional, you may have 10 feedback comments but not see the Detailed Seller Ratings yet because not all 10 buyers completed the Detailed Seller Ratings as well as leaving a feedback comment.

About Me Page

eBay gives you the option to create a page all about you. If you're a dealer, this will be all about your dealership.

Include photos, a bit about you and what you do, anything that personalizes you to your buyers. Talk about your classic car, or the dream car you are working toward affording. Try to identify with your buyers. This goes a long way to building trust.

If a buyer sees a new seller with under-10 feedback, but he has a personal About Me page, the buyer is more likely to buy from him. This page is also the only place on eBay that you can include a link to an outside website. So if you're a dealer, this is the place to put your dealership's website address.

To start an About Me page:

1. Go to www.ebay.com and click the Community tab (this is not visible on eBay Motors).

2. Scroll all the way to the bottom and click "Create an About Me Page" under the "More Community Programs" heading.

3. Upload photos and enter your text. You can also change the picture and text layout.

4. Once you're done, you'll get the About Me page icon next to your User ID (see Chapter 1). This lets all potential buyers know about your page just by glancing at your User ID in the Meet the Seller box.

It may take you a little bit of time to get set up as a seller, but it's well worth it. You can jump straight in without doing any of this, but you'll realize higher final values and more bids if you take the time to do it right.

Preparing to Sell Your Vehicle

Before you even consider listing your vehicle, you need to be sure you can actually sell it. If there is a lien on it, get a payoff amount for one month hence (allowing time for the auction duration and the buyer to send payment). Add $100 for eBay fees to that amount, and this is the lowest you can set your Reserve Price. Don't even think about running a no-reserve auction if you have a lien outstanding on the vehicle.

You will also need to get the title transferred to your bank's local branch. This is important because it can take up to two weeks after a loan is paid off for the title to be actually in the hands of the owner. You may be able to pay for overnight delivery, but it's far better to have it sent to the local branch (and confirm it is there) before you list the auction.

If you have already paid off your vehicle, good for you! Now you need to find the title. Be sure you know exactly where it is before listing the auction. If you can't find it, check with the bank you had your lien with. Sometimes they don't actually send it to you unless you request it. So they may still have it even though your lien is paid off.

You'll also want to get the maintenance records together. Many buyers will ask for them or details from them.

Sell Your Vehicle Checklist

eBay has a handy list for you to use before you start listing your item. It's available at pages.motors.ebay. com/sell/Sell_Your_Vehicle_Checklist.pdf.

I discuss many of the items on the checklist (and why they are important) in the next few chapters, but I highly recommend you print out this PDF document and use it whenever you list a vehicle.

The Least You Need to Know

- Credibility is everything. Get PayPal Verified and have a Confirmed Address to instill confidence in your buyer.

- Enroll in the Expanded Use Program or put your Social Security number on file with PayPal to remove the $500 a month withdrawal limit on your account.

- You will have to upgrade your PayPal account once you hit $500 in payments a month or 5 credit card transactions during 12 months.

- Estimate your eBay and PayPal fees before listing your auction so you can include them in your starting or Reserve price.

- Sell inexpensive items first to build your feedback.

- Create an About Me page to identify with your buyers and let them know a bit more about you.

8

Know Your Vehicle

In This Chapter

- Searching for specifications
- Avoiding value-dropping surprises
- eBay's research tools
- Finding online experts
- Researching the price

If you're a particular enthusiast of the vehicle you are selling, knowing the features and specific details about this model shouldn't be too difficult. If you don't live and breathe for that car, then you need to do a bit more research.

Either way, you'll need to check that you have the full specifications readily accessible to the buyer. There's nothing worse for a buyer than seeing a listing with an incomplete (or worse, inaccurate) vehicle description and specs list.

If there's one piece of advice I can give you, it is be an expert in anything you sell. This translates to everything you sell on eBay, whether it's on eBay

Motors or not. If you don't know the information, find out before you list the item.

Finding the Specs

Yes, a ridiculously long list of specifications that includes everything from floor mats to tilt-wheel is a bit of overkill. However, you should always include a specs list with the car's major features, for example, engine size, cruise control, power features, radio/CD player type, exterior/interior color, transmission, number of doors, keyless entry, etc. I talk about how to display this in Chapter 10, but for now, let's look at how you compile this information.

You are not expected to know it all; in fact, even if you do think you know it, it's still worth checking in case you forget something, or remembered it wrong.

You can find a wealth of information at the manufacturer's website, but these will usually only pertain to the current model year (or possibly the last couple of years). So if your vehicle is a few years old, you may need to look elsewhere. Some manufacturers have *VIN* lookup services.

This is a really cool feature because you just enter your VIN and it will display all the factory-built specifications. Now, if you've added after-market parts, these won't show up, but it should give you a good starting point.

Kelley Blue Book on eBay

For years, sellers have had to research vehicles through various online sources. Now, eBay has brought it all to you in one handy place. There is a new navigation tab at the top right of every eBay Motors page labeled "Research." This is where you can find out nearly everything about a vehicle.

Back in Chapter 2, we looked at the main category page for a particular make and model. Here we're going to look at the second tab, labeled "Specs & Photos."

To get to this page:

1. Click Research on the main navigation bar.

2. Select your vehicle's make and model using the drop-down menus.

3. Click on the Specs & Photos tab.

4. Select the Generation (if applicable).

5. Scroll down to the Year section and click "see all specs" beneath the correct year for your vehicle.

This takes you to the Specifications page. Here you can find almost everything you need to know about the vehicle. It is provided by Kelley Blue Book, which is one of the most trusted vehicle information and pricing sources on and off the web.

On the specifications page, you will find:

- EPA gas mileage for city and highway driving

- Engine type (V6, 4-cylinder, rotary, etc.)
- Drive wheel (front-wheel drive, etc.)
- Transmission options, including the number of gears (6-speed manual, automatic, etc.)
- Horsepower
- Dimensions for both exterior and interior, including height and legroom
- Factory warranty information
- Standard equipment on all vehicles of this model year; this is often called "stock" or "base" model
- Available equipment for upgrade options on this model year

To see the safety information (such as number and location of airbags), select a trim style. There may only be one option, but you will still need to select it to view this information.

There is a lot of extra information here that you really don't need to include in your listing. Frankly, if the buyer really wants it, he can look at the same research you have.

I recommend you print out the Available Equipment section and take a look at your car with the list in hand. Check off each item you have. You should be able to determine almost all of them just by looking at the car.

There are other websites that can give you similar information to the Kelley Blue Book research on eBay, such as www.edmunds.com and www.nadaguides.com.

Car Club Websites

Most popular cars have a website forum for owners. Here you will find a wealth of information. It's
really easy to find a forum for your vehicle model.
Go to your preferred search engine and enter the
make, model, and the word "forum." You'll get a
bunch of options, so browse through them until
you find one you like.

Reviews and Guides

There is a section on eBay called *reviews* and *guides*
that can be useful when you're researching a vehicle.
When you're looking for stock feature lists, you need
to look for reviews rather than guides.

def•i•ni•tion

Both **reviews** and **guides** are written by other
eBay members. Reviews are written about
products. Guides are written as "how-to"
information. So you might see a review for a
2008 Ford Mustang GT or a guide for how
to check a vehicle for flood damage.

The tab next to the Specs & Photos on the make/
model category page is labeled "Ratings & Reviews."
Clicking this takes you straight to the reviews other
eBay members have posted about this particular
vehicle.

Some reviews list stock specifications, or even the
upgrades attached to each model trim. This is not

verified information, so use it as a starting point, not as a definitive list.

Vehicle History Reports

The last thing you need is a buyer telling you about something he found on a vehicle history report that you didn't disclose in the auction. Either you look highly unprofessional for not doing your research, or you could be accused of deliberately omitting the information, which is misrepresentation, and a type of fraud. Neither is a good situation.

CARFAX and AutoCheck are the two main vehicle history report providers. I talked about them in Chapter 3 so refer there for the details of pricing and how to order the reports.

You should have obtained a vehicle history report when you bought the car (if you didn't buy it new). So you should already know what is on there, and what might have been added since you've owned the vehicle (such as any minor accidents or body work you've had done).

Still, it's worth getting another one now. They are not very expensive, and you can offer it to buyers in the listing and have them contact you if they are interested in seeing it. This has the advantage of starting a dialogue between you and the buyer, which helps make you more memorable.

Pricing Your Vehicle

This is the million-dollar (if you're lucky) question: how much should you list your vehicle for?

Every vehicle is different. They have different histories, different options, different mileage, etc. You have to take all this into account. My preferred method is the same for sellers as it is for buyers trying to find a good deal. Look at all the pricing sources and then average them.

eBay Price Research Tools

On the make/model category page, the fourth tab is labeled "Price Research." On this page you will see a box showing the price range of recent sales and the Kelley Blue Book suggested retail price (it's labeled "What It's Worth"). Bear in mind that this does not account for mileage, options, etc.

Clicking on the Just Sold link shows you the Completed Listings for this vehicle model and year. Remember, when you're looking at Completed Listings, the only ones you should be concerned with have prices in green. These were the ones that actually sold. If the price is red, it did not sell. You can click on any auction in the Completed Listings and see the full auction (so you can check how similar the specifications are to your vehicle).

On the Price Research page you can use the Kelley Blue Book Configurator to get a more accurate suggested price based on the mileage, options, condition, etc. Most buyers will be doing the same research you are, so if you price your vehicle over the suggested retail price, you're simply not going to get the bids.

Other Online Sources

I like Kelley Blue Book, but it is not the only price guide used in the industry. Some dealerships prefer to use NADA Guides (available online at www. nadaguides.com). I like NADA Guides because you have more optional equipment choices. So if you've made upgrades, you can see how that affects the price rather than guessing.

The other site I really like is Edmunds (www. edmunds.com). This site gives you a True Market Value (TMV), which tells you what consumers are actually paying for that vehicle in your area. Sure, this isn't as relevant when your buyers are out of state, but it will give you an indication of what you'd get for selling it locally. If you live near a major city, you'd be amazed at how many local buyers will find you through eBay Motors.

Remember, these suggested prices are what you *can* get for the vehicle; it doesn't mean that you *will* get that amount. This suggested price is a good place to set your Reserve Price or Buy It Now price. However, your starting price should be much lower to get bidders interested.

The Least You Need to Know

- Use the eBay tools available to you to find the vehicle specifications and prices.

- Search the forums on car club websites or post a question if you can't find the information you need elsewhere.

- Look at other listings to see how much information they offer, but don't copy them word for word.

- Get a vehicle history report so you know what you're selling.

Visuals That Sell

In This Chapter

- Photos that sell
- Making your photos better
- Photo angles and features
- Lighting and backgrounds
- Showcase your vehicle in video

In no other category does your picture sell your product more than eBay Motors listings. It only costs you $2.00 for 24 photographs, so it's worth making use of this to really show off your car. (All the picture services fees are outlined in Chapter 7.)

It doesn't matter if it's a 1990 Honda Civic or a restored 1970 Chevelle SS—the pictures will really make a huge difference to your listing and the price you get for your vehicle. Your job is to capture the essence that makes your vehicle better than any other.

Because of the uniqueness of each vehicle (based on condition, options, etc.), the buyer cannot go to a local store and check out the item you're selling before buying from you. So your pictures have to tell the buyer everything he needs to know about the vehicle, *and* get him fired up and enthusiastic about it.

Take Your Best Shot

Before I talk about *what* shots you need to take, I need to address *how* you should take them.

You will need a digital camera. Yes, you can use a regular 35mm and have a photo processing lab put the pictures onto a CD for you, but when you're taking pictures of a vehicle, you really need that instant review picture so you can look at it and be sure it is right. You don't want to have to reshoot it later.

Location, Location, Location

Sure, you could photograph your vehicle in your driveway, but if you want a picture with the added "wow" factor to grab buyers' attention, you'll need to go to a better location.

You may not be blessed with a spectacular view just a five-minute drive from your house, but I'm sure you know some pretty places. Even if it's in front of a park, it's better than a concrete parking lot or your driveway.

What Equipment You Need

A tripod is as essential as your digital camera. It prevents shakiness when you take the picture (particularly if you use the self-timer), and it allows you to alter something on or around the vehicle without having to set up the shot again.

You can pick up a used tripod for less than $10 on eBay, craigslist, or at a yard sale. This is the only other essential piece of equipment you'll need.

The Right Time to Shoot

You've got everything ready, now you need to decide when to take the pictures. This is largely decided for you based on where you live and what time of year it is.

Here are a few tips:

- Always wait for visible weather to stop (not raining, snowing, etc.).
- Don't shoot a white or gray car against a background of snow.
- If it's very sunny and your car has flaws in the paint, wait for some clouds, or shoot when the sun is not high in the sky.
- If you have perfect paint, shoot in the sun.
- Avoid dusk and dawn unless you can catch one perfect shot of your car with a beautiful sunset behind it. This can be used as one of your shots, but the others should all be in daylight.

Make the most of what you have.

Shooting Lessons

Even if you're not an avid photographer, you can take good photographs of your vehicle. There are just three simple steps:

1. Set up your shot so the area you want to capture fills the frame (what you're seeing on the LCD screen).

2. Turn off the flash.

3. Use the timer on your camera to take the shot. This way you won't risk moving the camera at all when you take the picture.

It's that simple. Yes, you can do much more, but if you have limited photography knowledge, this is the bare minimum you must do.

Turning off the flash prevents glare and helps mask flaws in paint. Because you're shooting outside in daylight, you shouldn't have any trouble with the image being too dark. If your interior seems too dark, try it with the flash and see which looks better.

If your camera is equipped with a "backlight" feature, this works very well to just fill in areas that need a little more light. Alternatively, your car's overhead light might be enough to remove the need for flash.

Photos and Angles You Should Use

This is the list of photos I would include of the exterior. This is in addition to close-up photos of any damage, windshield chips, scratches, etc.:

- Front of vehicle

This shot doesn't have to be straight on. You can use a bit of an angle as I have here to make it look a bit more interesting. I also turned on the headlights so I could show the upgraded halogen lights.

- Rear of vehicle
- Left side
- Right side

You may want to use some close-up shots of the doors if there is any damage, but this is an important shot to show the whole side of the vehicle.

- Wheels
- Side view from front corner showing whole vehicle; choose the best-looking side for this picture

This makes a really good gallery picture because it is interesting and shows more than one side of the vehicle.

- Engine bay (under the hood)
- Rear of car with trunk open
- Close-up of any after-market parts (new exhaust, body kit, etc.)

Don't forget photos of the interior:

- Dashboard showing gauges
- Front seats
- Back seats
- View from driver's-side door (open) looking into interior of vehicle
- Trunk space
- Stereo system (turned on)
- Close-up on the odometer
- Any cool features (navigation system, satellite radio, DVD player, etc.)

When you're taking close-up shots, turn on macro. This is a camera setting that keeps your photographs in focus even when you're zoomed in very close. Without it, your close-up shots may seem blurry. The icon for this option is a tulip flower on most cameras.

Detailing Tips

When adding a photo of a scratch or ding, use a common item to give the photo a sense of scale. Some sellers hold a dollar bill or a coin near the flaw; others may use a ruler or tape measure.

Specific information about photographing parts and accessories can be found in Chapter 14.

It's My Car ... Honestly!

There is so much you can do with computers these days. It would be very easy to edit your photographs and make the vehicle look better than it actually is.

Stop. You have to resist the temptation to do this. Yes, it's quite easy, but it's not the honest or right thing to do. For one thing, you'll end up with a very unhappy buyer when they see the actual vehicle, and you may find yourself in trouble with eBay if the buyer files a misrepresentation claim. It's just not worth it.

It's okay to fix glares, clean up the background around the vehicle, and adjust the brightness and/or color balance if it is inaccurate. None of these edits change the vehicle itself.

It is not okay to …

- Remove scratches or other flaws from the paint.
- Make the color look richer than it is.
- Add in any element that is not from your own vehicle.
- Smooth out paint or lines on the car to make it look better.

Honesty in pictures is very important. If you stick to these editing restrictions, you should be fine. If in doubt, look at the edited photograph next to the car. If the photograph makes it look better than the car actually is, then you were too heavy-handed in your editing.

Lights, Camera, Action!

Another option is to include a video clip in your auction. It has to be embedded (i.e., the video plays within the auction page), but that's not as hard as it sounds. A 360° tour of the vehicle can really help your buyer feel like he is looking at it in person, so this is worth considering.

I'm going to show you how to do this with YouTube as the video host, but you can use any of eBay's approved sites (available at pages.ebay.com/help/policies/listing-links.html).

First you have to upload it:

1. Film your video clip. It needs to be short, no more than a minute, or it won't load quickly enough on your auction page. Thirty seconds is even better.

2. Use whatever software came with your camera to transfer the file to your computer.

3. Go to www.YouTube.com and sign up for an account.

4. After you sign in, go back to the YouTube homepage and click Upload.

5. Fill out the details, including a title, description, and at least one keyword ("eBay motors" is a good choice here).

6. Select Autos and Vehicles from the Video Category drop-down menu and then click Upload a Video.

7. Click Browse to find the video on your computer, select it, and then click Open.

8. Click Upload Video to start the upload. This may take some time depending on the size of the video and the speed of your Internet connection. When you see a new page that says "Video Upload—Upload Complete," it's done.

Now, to get the video embedded into your auction:

1. Click on My Account (on YouTube) and then My Videos.

2. When you see the video show up in My Videos (it will be a gray box until it is fully processed), click on it and you'll see the full video page.

3. On the right side are two boxes. One says "URL" the other says "Embed." Both have coding text in them. Click on the text inside the Embed box and copy it to your clipboard (right-click your mouse and select copy).

4. Now navigate to the HTML Editor on the eBay Sell Your Item form (where you entered your description).

5. Locate where you want the video to display and hit Enter or Return five times so you have a good amount of extra space.

6. Click the "Enter your own HTML" tab at the top of the HTML Editor. This is going to look pretty scary if you've never seen HTML coding before. Just look for five consecutive lines that only say <P> <P> on each line. These are those five extra lines you entered in step 5.

7. Place your cursor after the first line and paste the text you copied from YouTube (right-click and select Paste).

8. Click the tab labeled "Standard" at the top of the HTML Editor. This puts you back to the view you are used to seeing and you'll see the video displayed in the page. Now you can delete those extra lines you put in.

9. Click the play button in the center of your video to be sure it plays correctly. If you just see a link here instead of the video, you copied the wrong coding from the YouTube page. Go back and copy the text from the other box, and repeat steps 4 through 9.

This sounds like a lot of work, but it's really worth it to showcase your vehicle. When the auction is over, you can remove the video from YouTube by clicking Remove next to the thumbnail image in My Videos on YouTube's website.

The Least You Need to Know

- Pick a scenic background to take your photographs against so your vehicle stands out and looks more appealing.
- Turn off the flash to avoid glare, and use the macro feature for close-up photography.
- Use a tripod and the timer feature to avoid blurriness and shakiness in your photographs.
- Avoid direct sunlight unless your paint is flawless. Cloudy weather is more forgiving.
- Don't over-edit your pictures. This is misrepresentation and a form of fraud.
- Showcase your vehicle with a short video clip.

10

Writing a No-Fluff Vehicle Title and Description

In This Chapter

- The structure of a good listing
- What to write and how to write it
- When blank space is more important
- Titles that get noticed

This is the part that most new sellers dread. Some choose to overcome this by just writing a one- or two-line description; however, this ultimately hurts them in the number of bids and the final selling price.

If you don't write a complete description, you'll find yourself with lots of buyer questions if you're lucky (and if you're not, the buyers will just move on to the next auction). Answering these questions takes far longer than if you'd just taken the time to write a good description in the first place.

I'm going to break it down into separate parts to make it much more manageable and less daunting.

Break Down the Description

I know logically, we should be looking at the title first because that is the order it is presented in the *Sell Your Item form*. However, it's much easier to write a title after the description is written.

def•i•ni•tion

The **Sell Your Item form** is the form you complete to list an auction. It includes fill-in-the-blank sections, select-from-a-menu sections, and the main section for writing your description.

There are seven parts to your description:

1. **Opening.** A one- or two-line "hook" that will grab the reader's attention and keep them on the page.

2. **Introductory paragraph.** A short paragraph covering the best features both of the model (horsepower, safety rating, etc.) and those unique to your vehicle (low mileage, upgraded parts, restored, etc.).

3. **The specs list.** A bulleted list of all the specifications (engine type, color, mileage, transmission type, optional equipment, etc.).

4. **About the model.** This is where you elaborate on the best model features and include more of them (incredible gas mileage, super-smooth handling, etc.).

5. **About your car.** Again, here you elaborate on the unique features of your car (condition, number of owners, warranty, etc.).

6. **Payment options.** eBay gives you a separate section for this, but it never hurts to repeat your specific payment requirements in the description.

7. **Shipping and handling.** Again, you'll have another section for this, but put the information in the description, too.

If you break down your description into these sections, it is much easier to write. Now you know the order; let's look at the content that goes into each of these sections.

Contented to Write Content

When you're writing your description, remember that there are three types of buyers: those who know exactly what they want, those who have a vague idea what they want, and those who have no clue.

You need to cater to all of them, so keep that in mind when you're choosing how to explain the vehicle features. Let's look at each section of your description in a little more detail with some examples.

I should stress that this is *my* preferred format and if you follow it, you won't miss anything in your description. However, you will see highly successful sellers who prefer to write their descriptions differently. I would start off using this format because I know it works, but as you get more experienced, you will probably want to modify it to suit your own style.

Opening

I like to use the make/model of the vehicle centered on the page in a large bold font (usually in blue because it stands out) and then beneath it, something amazing about the car: "J.D. Power Best in Class for Safety Ratings 5 Years Running!" or whatever. Then beneath that, in a smaller font (in red) I put the retail cost (assuming my price is well below that). This should all be centered on the page and boldface.

The purpose of this is to grab the reader's attention, tell them something they don't know about the vehicle, and make them want to read on. If you can catch your buyer with this, half your battle is won already.

I like to use dark blue, red, and black for my color scheme. I think it looks patriotic with the white background, but it also helps you accent certain areas of text without it looking gaudy. Don't go over the top with bright colors or use more than two variations, because you might come across like a "used-car salesman." Not a good first impression.

Detailing Tips

Use the dealer retail price in your listing description, not private party price. The difference is often thousands of dollars.

Introduction Paragraph

Keep up the enthusiasm. The only way to keep the buyer on your auction is to keep him interested. So use short, snappy sentences that convey emotion as well as the best features of the car.

Was it a show car, and if so, how many trophies has it won? Is it a restored classic with original parts? Has it been tricked out with NOS or other tuner features? Talk about the best model features, too. Does it have more than 200 horsepower? Has it won best in class awards or received particularly high safety ratings?

Don't list all the features, just the best few. I get to all the others later. Right now, you are just getting the buyer interested and reading on.

Think about how you would describe the vehicle to someone in person. You can use words like "smells like new" or "drives like a dream," which you don't usually see in formal writing. Writing in a familiar tone helps the buyer identify with and trust you. This is vitally important for your auction to be successful.

Try to avoid short, one-word sentences (manual. ST package. Spoiler. etc.). Instead, always write in full sentences. Always address the buyer: "*You* will love the Bose surround sound system."

Talk to your potential buyer as if he has already bought the car. Describe how it handles, the features you love (ignore the features you don't love), and get enthusiastic about it. This helps get the buyer enthusiastic. If you can make your reader imagine himself driving your car, you've pretty much assured yourself of a bid.

Sports cars are quite easy to get fired up about, but it's important to do this no matter what your vehicle is. Think about what the vehicle is designed for, and cater to that. Trucks are rugged, work-horse-type vehicles; sports cars are fun, sleek, and fast; SUVs are a mix of comfort and practicality ... you get the idea.

The Specs List

You should put the specifications into an easy-to-read bullet list like this:

- **Model:** RX-8
- **Style:** 4-door coupe
- **Package:** Sport touring
- **Transmission:** 6-speed manual
- **Color:** Velocity Red
- **Options:** Keyless entry
  Power driver and front passenger seats
  Power windows

Traction control system (can be turned on
and off with a switch)
Homelink mirror
Spoiler

Bulleted lists break up the rest of the text and make
it easier to find a specific feature in the list.

Most of this information is also used in the *Item
Specifics* when you create your listing, but many
buyers scroll past that section without looking at
it, so be sure to cover it in the main body of the
description as well.

def•i•ni•tion

Item Specifics help categorize items to
make it easier for the buyer to narrow down
his results to what he's really interested in. If
you don't complete them, your items won't
display if the buyer uses the eBay tools to
narrow down his results.

About the Model

In this section, you can elaborate on details of the
model. Include more details about the awards,
safety features, etc.

Remember, you are writing for both people who
know they want this vehicle, and people who are
still deciding what they want. Make a list of the
most important things most people want in a truck/
sports car/SUV/hybrid in general. Now look at the

features of your car and highlight those that match your list.

About Your Car

Here you need to give as much detail about your car and its history as possible. Cover the number of owners, existing warranty, maintenance records, etc. If you are linking to a CARFAX or AutoCheck report, this is the place to do it. Remember, this is all about why *your* car is better than the others of the same model year.

Payment Options

If you require a deposit (highly recommended), be sure you specify the amount here, as well as when it must be paid. You might want to say "if this may be a problem for you, please contact me prior to bidding and we'll see what we can work out." That way you're not excluding potential buyers who might take an extra day to get the deposit to you, and you're showing yourself as an approachable person who's willing to work with a buyer (always a good thing).

I recommend allowing loan checks, cashier's checks with a letter of guarantee from the bank, and escrow (through www.escrow.com). Escrow is the safest payment method so you might consider offering to split the cost with the buyer as an incentive for him or her to choose that option.

In Chapter 4, I talked about all the payment options, so refer to that section for more information about how each option works and how safe it is.

I always require a $500 nonrefundable PayPal deposit. Yes, you will pay fees on this ($14.80 if your monthly PayPal transactions are under $3,000), but I think it is worth it.

If the buyer didn't pre-arrange financing and is unable to follow through with the sale, you still get to keep the deposit. This covers the eBay and PayPal fees as well as some extra for the inconvenience of having to relist it. (See Chapter 13 for how to get some fees refunded and get a free relist.)

You'll select the time frame and deposit amount in the Payment Options section of the Sell Your Item form, but it's always worth reiterating it.

Shipping and Handling

You'll have a specific section for this in the Sell Your Item form, but it's worth putting it in the description as well. It is usually the buyer's responsibility to arrange shipping. You should clearly state that here.

You can offer other incentives, such as offering to drive the vehicle to the closest DAS or United Road terminal (two of eBay's preferred shippers). This saves the buyer a good amount of money, but be sure it's not too far from you.

If you still have a lien on the vehicle, you need to let the buyer know that and specify how long it will take from when you receive their payment to you being able to transfer the title. It should be same day the payment clears if you've done your preparation as outlined in Chapter 7. If not, you may have to pay your bank to overnight the title to you once the loan is paid off.

Closing

It's always worth adding a quick personal line at the bottom of the description reminding buyers that they can contact you if they need more information. Be aware of how you say it though. Look at the difference between these two phrases:

> E-mail with questions.

> If you have any questions, or need further photos, please don't hesitate to e-mail me.

The first is abrupt and doesn't really seem like the seller is actually welcoming questions. The second is far more polite and personal. It gives a much better impression of you to the buyer.

It's All in the Delivery

Okay, so we've looked at the organization and the content. Now let's look at the delivery. This is not *what* you say, but *how* you say it. I touched on this in the previous sections, but let's go into a bit more detail.

Make the Most of Your Car

You can't change the features and condition of your vehicle. However, you can change how you talk about it and the impression that gives the buyer. Look at the difference here:

> 2006 Red Mazda RX-8 ST. Manual. One non-smoking owner. Excellent condition. Leather interior. Seats 4.

Or:

> Stunning Velocity Red 2006 Mazda RX-8 with Sport Touring package. Let the quick, responsive, 232 H.P. rotary engine and 6-speed manual transmission unleash the "Zoom Zoom" in you.
>
> Flawless paint—waxed every weekend and parked in a garage. The super-clean interior comes complete with racing-style bucket seats covered in sleek two-toned red and black leather; a kicking Bose speaker system; and 6-disc, in-dash CD/MP3 player.
>
> I've won four trophies for this car so far this year.
>
> Superb safety features including a 5-star roll-over rating and 4-star impact rating on all sides. This is a safe sports car that your whole family can enjoy. The two bonus back seats (accessed using the reverse opening back door) are perfect for kids (and will fit a car seat with or without LATCH).

I'm the only owner (and a nonsmoker). Well maintained (records of all scheduled services available).

Remember, you are not limited on words, so get creative. Don't let your description read like a charged-per-word newspaper classified ad.

You'll notice in the second version I used a lot of adjectives—"stunning," "quick," "responsive," "super-clean," "sleek," "kicking," "bonus"—this is because these words convey emotion.

It's hard to describe "new-car smell" to a buyer the other side of the country, but by using well-chosen adjectives, you can convey your emotion about the car and pass it on to the buyer. This is something that sets apart the professionals on eBay Motors from the casual seller.

Go to the Completed Listings and look at the descriptions for the vehicles that sold for the highest amounts. I would bet that 9 out of 10 descriptions include good use of adjectives.

Colors of the Rainbow

One thing you might have noticed was my use of the phrase "Velocity Red." This is not just me coming up with a cool name (although I do think this is one of the best color names out there); this is actually a factory color for this vehicle.

You should find and include the factory color name if at all possible. Some buyers will look for it, but as shown earlier, the color name often helps sell your vehicle. Look at this list of official factory colors (from various manufacturers):

Velocity Red   Magnetic Blue

Screaming Yellow   Phantom Black

Performance White   Storm Titanium

Breakwater Blue   Highland Green

These evoke far more emotion than just red, yellow, green, white, black, etc. Each one gives an impression of the car, not just the color.

If you're selling painted parts (such as spoilers), it's critical to get the color name right. Many manufacturers have multiple blues or silvers. For Mazda, Galaxy Gray is different from Sunlight Silver, which is different from Titanium Gray or Liquid Platinum. Simply saying "silver" will not suffice. Buyers need to know exactly what color the item is painted to determine if it will match the rest of their vehicle.

Laying It All Out

Utilizing white space (the areas of the page that don't have any text or pictures in them) is important to the flow of your description and critical to keeping your reader interested. You've seen this on print ads thousands of times. There is a paragraph off-set with a picture, some callout lines, etc. You're a little more limited on your auction (unless you happen to be an HTML expert), but there are still things you can do.

I've mentioned using bullets. I use these in all my auctions, not just eBay Motors listings. They are great for calling attention to important features.

When you have a sentence that you want to call attention to, consider putting it on its own line and centering it on the page. You might try adding bold or changing the color as well. (Keep it in your color scheme and not too bright, or it will look tacky.)

These callouts are great for catching a reader's attention because there is so much white space around them.

eBay offers a Listing Designer feature (for a fee), which allows you to choose a theme and border for the entire auction. It also allows you to change how the photos are displayed. I talk more about this in Chapter 11.

Using headings can be another great way to break up text. I always use this for the specifications, payment options, and shipping and handling sections. You don't have to do it this way, but I make the heading a larger font and then bold and underline it. I also like to use a different color (usually dark blue) from the main text of the auction (black). This makes the whole auction look more professional and is easier for the buyer to read and refer to.

Whatever you decide to do with your description, make use of the HTML Editor. You can change the color, size, font, alignment, and much more using it. Always preview your changes so you can see how it looks on a full screen (rather than in the little editor window).

Honesty and Ethics

I talked about editing photos in Chapter 9 and being careful not to go too far. The same is true with your words. Creative license allows you to use some flowery language, but does not allow you to change the facts. For example, saying "flawless paint" when you have dings or paint chips is misrepresentation.

Have someone else (who has seen the car) read over your description before you post it, just to be sure you didn't go too far. At the end of the day, you don't want an unhappy buyer who thinks you deliberately misrepresented the vehicle. This will only land you in a world of difficulties. So be sure that what you write is accurate, complete, and cannot be misinterpreted.

Always identify any flaws. If there are dings, photograph them and refer to the picture in your text. The more honest and up-front you are, the more likely you are to get a bid and a happy buyer.

Make the Most of Your 55 Characters

Okay, now we're ready to look at the title. This is the gateway to your auction. It doesn't matter how good a description you've written or photos you've taken, if your title doesn't entice the buyer, he will not click through to see the rest. Your title is what gets your listing read. You have 55 characters, so make them count.

Keywords That Buyers Search

A lot of shoppers find vehicles by searching key-words rather than browsing the category. In your title, you have room for 55 characters, which you can use wisely or foolishly. If you waste your characters on words no one searches for, they will not find your vehicle.

If you browse from eBay Motors to Mazda to RX-8 you'll find the search results all have "Mazda: RX-8" under the Make/Model heading. Under the Year heading, you'll see the respective year of each car. That information is automatically added when you enter the VIN of your car on the Sell Your Item form. All those terms (Mazda, RX-8, and the year) are searchable keywords and are equal to any word in your title. In other words, you do *not* need to repeat those words in your 55-character title.

There are two purposes to the title. First, it should include keywords that buyers search so your listing shows up in the results. And second, it should grab the interest of the buyer when he scans either the category page or the search results page.

Don't forget you've already got "Mazda," "RX-8," and "2006" automatically included in your keywords, so you do not need to repeat them. If your model is under 12 characters, then you can put that in your submodel (I'll talk about that in a moment), but if it's long (like Sport Touring), you will need to find space in your title because it won't fit in the Sub Model section.

Think about what terms you would search for, but don't forget the phrases buyers are drawn to when they're scanning the results. Words and phrases like: "low miles," "premium wheels," "Upgrade," "smoke free," "clean," "flawless," "no reserve (or NR)," and "loaded."

Be sure it reads easily. If it reads like a jumble of keywords, try changing the order until it reads better. Remember, the buyer still has to want to click on it once it's shown up in the results. Here's an example:

> Red Sport Touring 6-Spd Manual LOW MILES w/ Navigation

For years, buyers have said the most important thing to them when choosing a new car is the color. Yet many eBay Motors sellers don't think of this when creating their title. If you have room, add the color as a keyword.

You can also use extra spaces to create white space between words. Remember how I talked about this for the description; it works here in the title too. Most sellers don't use this technique, so your title will stand out simply because the buyer catches that there is something different. He may not even realize what it is, but he's noticed your auction and is reading your title because of it. Here's an example of the original 51-character title:

> RED RX-8 RX8 ST 6-SPEED MANUAL NAVIGATION LOW MILES

And a couple different ways of using the extra four characters:

> RED RX-8 RX8 ST 6-SPEED MANUAL NAVIGATION LOW MILES
>
> RED RX-8 RX8 ST 6-SPEED MANUAL NAVIGATION * LOW MILES *

Check Engine

Be sure you put a space between the asterisk and the actual word; otherwise, a buyer searching for that word won't see your auction (the search engine treats the asterisks as part of the word if they are directly next to the word).

It's much better to use extra characters for another keyword or adjective, but if you've only got three or four characters left, using asterisks or extra spaces to highlight a keyword is much better than not using those characters at all.

Why Can't I Use a Subtitle?

eBay Motors vehicle listings already have two lines (the Make/Model and then the listing title you wrote). So you don't get an option of having an additional subtitle line.

When you enter the VIN for your vehicle, it will automatically insert the make and model; however, on the Sell Your Item form, there is an optional box labeled "Sub Model." Here you have an additional 12 characters that will display directly to the right of the make and model, above your title on the results page. So your Sub Model could say: Sport 6-Spd, ST 6-Speed, 10k Miles, Salvage, or Rebuildable. (I talk about selling salvage vehicles in Chapter 14, but both "salvage" and "rebuildable" are heavily searched keywords.)

This is basically like getting a subtitle for free. You'll still want to include most of the information in the actual title, but this is a good place to highlight one or two features that will grab the reader's attention. Have a look at cars similar to the one you are selling and see what words jump out at you. These are the ones to use (as long as they apply to your vehicle).

The Least You Need to Know

- Good auction descriptions are thought out and planned rather than rambling text.
- Use adjectives to help describe the vehicle in a more appealing way, but don't go too far and cloud the facts.
- Always use the official factory paint color, particularly if selling painted parts.
- Make your title keyword rich but also readable for buyers scanning the auction titles on the results page.
- Use layout, bullets, and color to make your auction look more appealing and keep the buyer's attention.
- Use the Sub Model box to get a free 12-character subtitle.

Listing Your Vehicle

In This Chapter

- Using the Sell Your Item form
- Critical information
- Getting help with the design
- Responding to questions
- Canceling a listing

In the previous chapter, I talked about two areas of the Sell Your Item form—the title and description. Now we're going to start at the beginning and look at each section and how to complete it to give the maximum impact.

To get to the Sell Your Item form from eBay Motors:

1. Click the Sell tab at the top right of any page.
2. Click Sell Your Item.
3. Sign in. (This is a security measure to be sure nobody unauthorized is listing auctions under your account.)

To Auction or Not?

Your first decision in the selling process is deciding on the selling format.

Your options are:

- Sell item at online auction
- Sell at a Fixed Price

You've heard me talking about Buy It Now before. The Fixed Price listing is strictly Buy It Now only. There is no starting price, just the selling price. When a buyer clicks Buy Now, the listing ends and that user is the winner. You also have the option to use *Best Offer* if you list at a Fixed Price.

def•i•ni•tion

> **Best Offer** allows buyers to submit an offer lower than your Buy It Now price. You can choose to accept the offer, reject it, or counter offer. You can auto-reject offers below a certain amount so you don't have to deal with buyers who are low-balling you.

If you are planning to use Best Offer, factor it into your Buy It Now price. So if you're willing to accept $9,000, you could set the Buy It Now price at $10,500, so you have room to haggle down (just like dealerships do).

Regular Online Auctions also have the option of a Buy It Now price. This is in addition to the starting price. Currently, eBay is testing keeping the Buy It Now price visible even after the first bid is placed. (Until now the Buy It Now option disappeared as soon as the first bid over the reserve price was placed.)

Right now the testing is in the Parts and Accessories category, and a few select others, but I expect Cars and Trucks will ultimately be included as well.

When you've made your selection for the selling format, click Continue.

Now you need to select your category. This is much easier on eBay Motors than the rest of eBay because there is no guesswork. You select your main category (Cars and Trucks, Parts and Accessories, etc.) and then select from the subcategories that appear in the second, third, and sometimes fourth, boxes. For example, if you're selling a Ford Mustang, your selection would be: Cars and Trucks—Ford—Mustang. It's as simple as that. After you've selected your category, click Continue.

Now you're on the first main page of the form. The first box is the title. You already have this written (from Chapter 10), so simply enter it here.

Item Specifics

This is one of the most important parts of the Sell Your Item form. When we looked at searching for vehicles in Chapter 2, one of the techniques we used was narrowing down the results using the options at the top of the page. This is pulled directly from the Item Specifics. I've said this before, but it warrants repeating—if you (the seller) don't fill out these optional fields, then your items will not show up when a buyer narrows down the results (even if your item would be a match).

Some of these are optional, others are required. You can't get past this page without completing all the required fields (marked with **).

Submodel. This is the free 12-character subtitle I talked about in Chapter 10. Make use of it by highlighting the submodel, the options or appearance package, or just one of the best features of the vehicle.

**Year. The model year of the vehicle.

**Vehicle Identification Number (VIN). This is required only if your vehicle model year is 1981 or newer so the buyer can run a CARFAX or AutoCheck vehicle history report. If your vehicle is 1980 or older, you should still include the VIN for full-disclosure purposes.

**Mileage. Pull this from your odometer when you list the item.

**Exterior Color. Use the drop-down menu to select the closest match. You'll include the exact factory color in the description.

Interior Color. This is optional, but worth including.

**Number of Cylinders. If you're not sure how many cylinders your vehicle has, look in your owner's manual (under Engine Specifications).

**Transmission. Select from Automatic or Manual.

Body Type. Optional, but worth including. Choose from Sedan, Coupe, SUV, Convertible, Pickup Truck, etc.

Cab Type. If you selected Pickup Truck for the Body Type, you'll have the option to select a cab type as well.

**Condition. Choose from Used, New, or Certified Pre-Owned.

**Is There an Existing Warranty? If yes, you must specify the details in your description.

**Type of Vehicle Title. This is very important. If you say it is Clear and it's not (i.e., it has a junk, salvage, or rebuilt title), you are committing fraud. Your options are Clear, Salvage, or Other. If you select Other, you must be specific about the title type in your description.

Vehicle Inspection. Only select if the vehicle has been inspected recently and you can prove it.

Options. Check the boxes for each of the options your vehicle has. Use the information you gathered for your specifications list (as explained in Chapter 10).

Fuel Type. Most vehicles are diesel or gasoline, but if you have some other fuel type, specify it here.

For Sale By. Select Private Seller or Dealer.

The Item Specifics should only take a minute or two to complete because you've already compiled most of the information for your description.

Driver's Ed

A clear title simply means it has never been written off as a total loss. A minor fender-bender or something similar that will show up on a CARFAX report does not affect the "cleanliness" of your title. If you're in doubt, look at the title. It will specifically say on it if it is anything other than clear.

Item Description

You can copy and paste the description you pre-wrote (per Chapter 10) straight into the HTML Editor box, or type it in if you prefer.

One of the options in the HTML Editor is Inserts. This allows you to insert a link to your other items or for the buyer to add you to his or her favorite sellers. This is particularly worth doing if you are a parts and accessories seller because you'll likely get more repeat buyers than vehicle sellers.

Don't forget to spell check and preview your description. When you're done, click Continue to move onto the next page in the Sell Your Item form.

Pricing and Duration

The next section is quite easy if you did your research and preparation earlier. In Chapter 8, we looked at how to price your vehicle. Here is where you enter that price.

In this section you can set three different prices:

Starting price. The minimum for the first bid.

Reserve price. The minimum you are willing to sell the vehicle for. (This is not displayed on the auction.)

Buy It Now price. The fixed price amount you are willing to sell the vehicle for now. If the buyer uses this option, the auction ends immediately and that person is the winning buyer.

The starting price isn't as critical on eBay Motors as it is on the rest of eBay, but you still want to be well below the competition (assuming you're using a Reserve). A rule of thumb some sellers use is to start the bidding at 10 percent of the Reserve price (i.e., $1,500 for a $15,000 vehicle). This gets the action started and gives the auction "velocity."

Reserve the Right Not to Sell

There are very few instances when I recommend *not* using a Reserve Price on a vehicle auction. If you're selling parts and accessories and did your price research properly, you'll likely be okay. But for vehicles, reserves are usually a must, particularly if you still have a lien on it.

If the bidding doesn't reach your reserve price, you can still offer a *Second Chance Offer* to any of your bidders.

def•i•ni•tion

Second Chance Offer allows you to offer to sell the item to a nonwinning bidder of your auction. It may also be used when the winning bidder backs out of the sale.

On eBay Motors, you can modify the price for a Second Chance Offer up to, but not over, your reserve price. You can send offers to any non-winning bidders of your auction. If a bidder accepts the offer, all the others will be automatically cancelled.

Giving to Charity

In this section of the Sell Your Item form, you also have the option to donate a portion of your proceeds to charity. This is eBay's *Giving Works* program.

def•i•ni•tion

eBay's **Giving Works** is a program that allows sellers to donate a portion of the final selling amount to the charity of their choice.

eBay will refund you the same proportion of your eBay fees that you gave to charity. So if you donated 25 percent of the proceeds of your auction to the American Red Cross, eBay would credit you 25 percent of your Insertion and Final Value Fees for that auction. There is a $5 minimum donation. For more information about Giving Works, go to givingworks.ebay.com.

Duration and Location

Now you need to select the duration of the auction. Your options are 3, 5, 7, or 10 days. You will pay an extra $8.00 for a 10-day listing, so I tend to avoid this option. Most people stick with a seven-day auction. For $1.00, you can have eBay launch the auction for you on a specific date and at a specific time.

Many people shop for vehicles on the weekend, so no matter when your listing ends, try to run it over a weekend.

Keep an eye on major events (such as the Super Bowl) that draw people away from their computers. Avoid listing over these times if possible.

Your item location is the next box. It defaults to wherever you are registered. If the vehicle location is different, be sure to change this. It's important because many buyers perform a distance search to see which vehicles are closest to them. If your vehicle is at a location other than your own, you may be missing out on potential buyers.

Adding Pictures

The first time you do this, you may need to download a file for the Enhanced Picture Services to work. It's worth accepting the download because then you can see thumbnails of each photo you've uploaded and in what positions they will display. The first box is your Gallery picture (the thumbnail that will show on the search results page). This should be the best picture you have that really shows off your car.

To upload a picture:

1. Click Add Pictures.
2. Locate the picture you want to upload from your computer and click Open.

To remove a picture:

1. Click on the picture so you see the large version on the right side of the box window.
2. Click Remove Pictures.

If you don't want to (or can't) use Enhanced Picture Services, you can switch to the second tab, which is Basic Picture Services. This won't give you the preview picture.

To upload using Basic Picture Services:

1. Click Browse.
2. Locate and select your picture.
3. Click Open.

The third tab is Your Web Hosting. If you're using a non-eBay host for your pictures, this is the option to use. You can use free picture hosting sites or even link straight from your website (particularly if you're part of a dealership that already has pictures of the vehicle online). You can select the URL for the gallery picture so you don't miss out on that. The Picture Services fees do not apply if you are using your own web hosting.

Listing Designer

In Chapter 10, I talked about text layout and mentioned that Listing Designer allows you to change the look of your auction. You can choose from many borders to go around your auction, but you need to be careful because some of them can actually detract from your description. There are a few eBay Motors–specific templates, and these seem to be a little better than the general ones.

The other feature of Listing Designer is changing how the pictures display (called picture layout). On the rest of eBay, there are five options. However, because most eBay Motors listings have lots of photos, there are only three options here.

My favorite option is Supersize Photos and Thumbnails. But because you pay an extra $5 for the use of the Listing Designer, it's not really worth it unless you're planning to use a border as well. The Standard default option is my second choice anyway.

Picture Layout Options

   Standard

   Supersize Photos and Thumbnails

   Supersize Photos

I'm not a big fan of the Supersize Photos layout because it detracts too much from the text. If you've got a car that sells itself (such as a restored 1969 Convertible Chevy Camaro), then the Supersize Photos layout might be good. But otherwise, stick to the other two options.

Why Pay for Listing Upgrades?

eBay has to make its money somewhere. Here is where most of it comes from. You've heard me talking about some of the upgrades you can pay for (such as Listing Designer, Scheduled Listing, etc.).

Now you have to select (or not) the other options you want to pay for.

Check Engine

Be careful—listing upgrade fees add up very quickly. They are much higher for eBay Motors than for the rest of eBay.

Bold ($4). Your title will display in boldface.

Highlight ($5). The area behind your title will be highlighted in light purple.

Border ($4). Your title and thumbnail picture will have a dark purple border surrounding. (This feature is usually used in conjunction with Highlight.)

Listing Icon ($2). This puts an icon to the right of your title to draw attention to it. The options are: U.S. flag, checkered flag, 4×4, gift box, or V8 icon.

Featured *Plus!* ($19.95). Places your auction in the Featured Items section at the top of the page.

Motors ProPack ($29.95). Combines Bold, Border, Highlight, and Featured *Plus!* You only save $3, so it's not worth it unless you were planning to use all these features anyway.

Motors Home Page Featured ($99.95). Gives you the chance to have your auction rotate to the main eBay Motors home page featured section. It may also appear in the featured listings of any other main pages. So a home page–featured BMW Z4 listing may appear on the main BMW page, the sports car page, or the BMW Z4 page. This is a very expensive option unless you have a very unique or highly desirable vehicle. The fee to home page feature a nonvehicle listing is $24.95.

I like to use Bold for most auctions. Depending on what I'm selling, I use Highlight and Border as well. It pays to look at the other auctions on the page, though. If all the items are using Bold, then being the only one *not* using this feature will actually make yours stand out more (and save you $4). Look at the features the other auctions are using and then decide what will make yours stand out among them.

Do a search for the vehicle you are listing and see how many competitors you have. If it's more than 100, take a look at how many of them are above the "Featured Listings" line. If a relatively small number are feature listings, you should consider that option to make your listing stand out in such a large crowd. Paying $19.95 may seem steep, but don't forget you're selling a high-ticket item and that extra exposure can get you more bidders.

The final option on this page is the page counter. This shows you (and everyone else unless you hide it) how many people have viewed your auction. These are unique users, not repeat views.

If you find that you're getting a lot of viewers but no bidders, you might want to change something in your description. If you're not getting the viewers, then your title probably needs some tweaking. (I explain how and when you can do this in Chapter 13.)

Click Continue to get to the next page. (You're almost done, I promise!)

Payment Options

I talked about this in Chapter 10. Be sure the information you enter here matches what you put in your description.

I highly recommend a PayPal deposit. The usual amount is $500, but you can adjust that higher or lower as you want. You can also specify if it is refundable, and how long the buyer has to make that payment. The default is 48 hours.

If you're using a Fixed Price Listing, you can require the deposit to be paid immediately. This will show on the auction listing page as "immediate PayPal deposit required." As soon as the buyer clicks Buy Now, he will be taken to a PayPal page to sign in and send you your deposit. He cannot buy the item without sending the payment.

I could go into a lot of detail about the Sell-to locations, but it can be summed up in two points:

- Don't sell vehicles to overseas buyers (unless you happen to live near the Canadian border and the buyer wants to pick it up).

- Be wary of selling parts to overseas buyers. Always require PayPal payment, and never send to an unconfirmed address.

I have my Sell-to locations set to United States only for eBay Motors items over $200. This is because fraud is much more prevalent in cross-border trans-actions. The amount of money at stake is just too high to risk it.

There are only three more sections on this page. The next is Buyer Communications. If you choose to use Skype (which allows you to be contacted by buyers through your computer via instant message or by voice-call through your computer), here is where you make your selections.

I have to admit, I'm not set up on Skype. I would rather have buyers e-mail me so I can e-mail them back on my schedule. When I'm working on non-eBay things, I don't want instant messages popping up from buyers when I'm trying to focus on some-thing else. Still, many sellers love it. I've used it for non-eBay communications, and it works very well.

The next section is Pickup and Shipping. Ninety-nine percent of the time, the buyer is responsible for organizing and paying for the shipping. The other option tells buyers to look at the description for details.

If you are offering any other service (such as driving to a terminal), but the buyer is still paying for it, I suggest you select the first option and just elabo-rate in the description.

The final section is the Buyer Requirements. This is worth using because it saves you a lot of frustra-tion. You can block bidders who are registered in countries you don't ship to (in this case, all non-U.S. buyers). You can also block bidders who've had two or more unpaid item strikes in the last month. This can help you avoid a nonpaying bidder (or someone who's had his account hijacked). Click Edit Preferences to the right of the section to modify the current selections.

Click Continue when you're done to go to your preview page. Here you can check all aspects of your auction and the options you have selected. It is also where eBay tries one more time to get you to choose listing upgrades.

When you're happy that your auction is ready to go, click Submit Listing. If you used Scheduled Listing, it will launch at the time you set. If not, it will get in the queue to upload as soon as possible. This may take an hour or more at peak times or during scheduled maintenance, so don't worry if you don't see it immediately.

You can track your auction and see the number of people watching it in My eBay.

CARad Express Listing Designer

In 2003, eBay purchased the Texas-based company CARad. This company specializes in assisting dealers launch and manage their vehicle auctions. They also have an express version for individuals (i.e., nondealers).

The fee is $9.95 per listing, but that includes the hosting for up to 35 photos and their templates, so if you subtract the fees eBay charges for these two features ($2 for the picture hosting and $5 for listing designer), the remainder is only $2.95. That's not bad. So if you were planning to use both of these eBay features anyway, you might find CARad Express a useful option. It certainly makes your auction look more professional. Go to express. carad.com for more details and to sign up.

The Least You Need to Know

- Complete all the Item Specifics, even if they are not required.
- Spell check and proofread everything.
- Use Giving Works to donate a percentage of your final price to the charity of your choice.
- Choose listing upgrades wisely because the fees add up quickly.
- Require a deposit via PayPal to get the buyer's confirmed address.
- Use CARad Express if you'd like to design a more professional listing.

12

Managing Your Auction

In This Chapter

- Responding to questions
- Ending a listing
- What if you're asked to sell off eBay?
- Vehicle inspections
- Correcting mistakes

Now that your listing is active, you can do one of two things: ignore it until the end, or proactively manage your auction.

Obviously, I recommend you do the latter. You will likely get questions from buyers, plus you'll get some people trying to get you to sell it off eBay, so you need to know how to handle this.

Responding to Questions

However well you write your auction description, you will get questions. Sometimes buyers (usually the savvy ones) ask you a question just to see how you respond. It's like a test.

You can have a professional design your listing for you, but it will likely be you answering the e-mails, so leaving a good impression is vital.

It may be a little frustrating, particularly if you have to answer the same question repeatedly, and the information is in the listing, but you must always stay polite. This is your test in customer service. Here are a few tips:

- Always write in full sentences, and use capital letters and correct punctuation. Proofread and spell check it before you send. Nothing says "I don't care" as much as a badly written e-mail.

- Be polite and helpful, never aggressive or snippy.

- Have a polite sign-off (like, "if you have any further questions, don't hesitate to e-mail me back").

- If you can't comply with a request (such as 20 more photographs) explain why, and offer a compromise.

- Check e-mail at least twice a day, and more frequently on the last day of the auction.

- *Never* ignore an e-mail. A buyer who doesn't get a response to a question will not bid on your auction.

You don't need to write an essay. In fact, getting too familiar with someone could take up valuable time you need elsewhere, but being polite and helpful goes a long way.

When Is It Okay to End a Listing?

Dealers always have a "get-out" clause, which says that the auction may be ended at any time due to local sale. You can do the same thing. One of the options you can select when you end a listing early is "the item is no longer available for sale."

As long as you've got more than 12 hours remaining on your auction, this is fine. However, you cannot end an auction within the last 12 hours if your listing has a winning bid or the Reserve has been met. You still pay the Insertion fee if you cancel the auction, but you won't have to pay the Transaction fee.

Other reasons that are acceptable for ending an auction early are …

- You made a major error in the listing and you already have a bid (so you can't correct it).
- The vehicle was damaged after you launched the auction and it is no longer in the condition you stated it was.

It is not okay to cancel an auction because …

- You didn't use a Reserve and the bidding didn't go as high as you wanted.
- A buyer who saw your eBay auction contacts you and wants to buy it off-eBay.

There is a distinction between a local buyer seeing your ad in AutoTrader or Craigslist and wanting to buy it, and an eBay buyer wanting to do the transaction off eBay.

Responding to Off-eBay Inquiries

So what do you do if you are approached by a buyer wanting to buy your vehicle off eBay? Well, the first thing that should happen is you hear alarm bells ringing. The buyer will lose all fraud protection if he doesn't complete the sale through eBay, so why would he want to do that?

You won't be able to verify his contact information through eBay either because you won't technically have been involved in a transaction together. Equally, you need to be wary of his feedback rating, too. If he makes a habit of this, there is no recourse for eBay sellers to warn other sellers because you can't post feedback if the transaction was not completed on eBay.

Having said that, some buyers may be genuine and trying to save you the Transaction fee, or jump ahead of other buyers. So you don't want to treat it as fraud and report the person unless it's very obvious.

Often you will have local buyers contact you to come look at the vehicle. They may offer to buy it from you on the spot. It's up to you. Technically, if they found you through eBay, it is against the terms and conditions to cancel the auction and sell directly to this buyer. However, this does happen a lot.

To be clear—I'm not condoning canceling auctions for this reason, I'm just stating that it does occur. I think going through eBay is the better option even if the buyer is local, because then you get credit for the transaction (through feedback). If you are trying to establish yourself as an eBay Motors seller, then you really need to get the feedback that reflects all the transactions you've done.

If your buyer isn't local, or hasn't inspected the vehicle in person, then don't even consider selling off eBay. This is where most of the scammers catch sellers.

They will have weird requests that mean you can't wait the usual time for payment to clear, or they will want to wire money directly to your bank (which requires you to give them your bank details), either of which could be a scam. Just don't do it. Decline politely, stating that you would prefer to complete the transaction through eBay.

If you don't have any bids on the auction, you can add a Buy It Now price for the offer he gave you, so the buyer can purchase it immediately, but you're still going through eBay. If the buyer really wants the vehicle, he'll bid.

Independent Vehicle Inspections

It isn't unusual for a buyer to want an independent inspection. In fact, there is nothing preventing you as the seller from ordering one. SGS Automotive Services is the company eBay recommends. It provides a 150-point inspection report online, usually within 24 hours of the inspection. Here are some typical questions and answers:

What type of vehicles will SGS inspect?

Most vehicles newer than 1980 model year. This includes sedans, SUVs, collectible and exotic vehicles, pickup trucks, motorcycles, and vans.

Do I have to allow an inspection?

No, the buyer must get your permission. However, you are certainly losing a potential buyer if you refuse. The buyer is obviously serious about bidding or he wouldn't be planning to pay almost $100 for an inspection.

How do I order an inspection for a vehicle I'm selling?

Call 1-800-806-0868. SGS is open Monday through Friday between 8 A.M. and 9 P.M. Eastern Time. Get the inspection done before you launch your auction so you can include the inspection report link right from the beginning.

What does it cost and how do I pay?

Most vehicles are $99.50, and you (or the buyer) pay via PayPal.

Do I have to be present for the inspection?

Yes, either the owner of the vehicle or an authorized representative over 18 years old must be present to sign the authorization agreement.

What will I need to have with me?

You need to show proof of vehicle registration and insurance at the time of the inspection (unless the vehicle is at a dealership, in which case dealer plates are sufficient).

When will the inspection take place?

It is usually scheduled for the day following the payment being received.

Will I know in advance that a buyer has ordered an inspection?

Yes, the buyer is required to notify you before ordering an inspection. He has to give SGS your contact information, which he can only get directly from you, so you won't get a call out of the blue from SGS.

How long does the inspection take?

Usually it takes 45 to 60 minutes. However, it may take longer for exotic or high-end luxury vehicles.

How long does it take to get the report after the inspection is completed?

Usually it takes 24 hours.

What will SGS do?

SGS inspects the exterior, interior, under the hood and under the vehicle, and takes digital photographs of it. It may also perform a short test drive.

Where can I get a full list of the 150 points SGS inspects?

Go to sgs-ebay.sgsauto.com/150_points.htm.

An extra hundred bucks for an independent inspection sounds like a lot, but if you have a pricey vehicle or there is a lot of competition on eBay for that particular model, having an independent inspection ready for the buyer can give you the edge. This could translate into thousands of dollars in extra bids, so it's well worth considering. You can read more about SGS Automotive Services inspections at: sgs-ebay.sgsauto.com/index.htm.

Handling Listing Errors

If you make an error, enter the wrong mileage, or mix up the features, don't panic. You don't have to cancel the auction. If there are no bids, you can modify the listing by clicking Revise Your Item from the auction page. As well as the title and description, you can modify the starting price, Reserve price, or add a Buy It Now price.

If you already have bids, you can click Revise Your Item and add extra information. So if there is a minor error, you can clarify it, or you can add something you originally forgot to mention. However, your bidders do have the option of retracting their bid if the change you make significantly alters the item.

The Least You Need to Know

- Always answer buyer questions fully using complete sentences and a polite tone.
- It's okay to end a listing early if a non-eBay buyer sees a local ad for your vehicle, but it is not okay if an eBay buyer approaches you to sell the vehicle outside eBay.

- Always allow buyers to order an independent inspection of your vehicle. Paying for an independent inspection before you list a vehicle gives you and your item instant credibility.

- You can revise your price, title, or description before you have a bid. After you have a bid, you can add to the description, including photographs, but you cannot remove anything.

Post-Auction Antics

In This Chapter

- Shipping a vehicle
- Damage in transit
- Transferring a title out of state
- When your buyer can't get financing
- If your vehicle doesn't sell

If you followed the tips I've outlined throughout this book, you shouldn't be plagued with PSB (Post-Selling Blues). However, there are a few things you need to be aware of after you have a winning bidder.

Preparing for Shipping

It is the buyer's responsibility to arrange for shipping. There is wisdom in letting the buyer choose the shipping company. If anything goes wrong along the way, they cannot blame it on your poor choice. It's up to you how helpful you want to be. As I've mentioned before, you might want to offer to deliver it to a carrier's terminal, but this is by no means a requirement. One thing that is a requirement is preparing the vehicle for shipping.

When the buyer has booked the shipping service, you should be able to get their list of instructions for vehicle preparation. These are the basics, but some carriers have other requirements as well:

- Be sure the fuel tank is ¼ full. No more, no less.

- Empty everything out of the vehicle (you should have done this anyway).

- Clean it from top to bottom (so the check-in person can see if there is any existing damage).

- Send the title separately, not in the glove compartment. Send maintenance records separately, too. The only thing in the glove compartment should be the wheel lock and the owner's manual. You may choose to send those separately, too.

Take photographs of the car at the terminal, or when the inspector does the inspection. Be sure to get photographs of any damage he notes. This way, if the damage is more extensive when it is delivered, it can't be blamed on you not disclosing it fully in the auction.

If you aren't automatically given a copy of the inspection report, request one. Don't let the shipper take the vehicle until you have this.

Make a copy of the inspection report, and send the original to the buyer (along with the title, etc.). The buyer will need it when he receives the vehicle to be sure it matches what the shipper has marked down on his copy. You might want to put the photos you took of the vehicle onto a CD and mail that, too. Be sure you keep a copy of everything for your records though.

Shipping Damage

As heartbreaking as this might be for you if this was a car you really liked, it isn't your problem. The buyer was responsible for arranging shipping. The shipper is responsible for the condition it arrives in if it is different from when it was picked up.

This is why you need to have photographic records as well as the inspection report. If there is any question of the condition when it was picked up, you have proof available. The shipper should cover the cost of the damage (if the buyer obtained insurance coverage through them) or, if not, the buyer's auto insurance should cover it (assuming he followed my tips in the buying chapters and had the vehicle added to his insurance before having it shipped). It is not your responsibility, and your insurance will not cover it (nor should they), even if the buyer doesn't have any insurance to pay for the damage.

Having said that, your feedback will suffer if you aren't helpful. Be sure to offer all the documentation you have to the buyer and/or his insurance company. Even if you sent it already, making an extra copy and putting it in the mail takes you only a few minutes, and it could make a huge difference for the buyer.

But do not let anyone bully you into believing that you are responsible for the vehicle. As long as you prepared the vehicle to the shipper's requirements, once you handed it over, it stopped being your problem.

The only time this could be an issue is if the money was held in escrow. Most buyers will understand that it's still your money and it's not your fault, but some may try to be difficult, particularly if the title has not been transferred yet.

The closed eBay auction page is your bill of sale. It is a legally binding contract. If you have to fight to get your money, this is your proof. You have photographs of the condition it was sent in and a bill of sale. That should be enough to get the funds released.

Out-of-State Title Transfers

Every state has slightly different requirements and procedures. If you're selling to an out-of-state buyer, you need to check the requirements for both states. The easiest way to do this is to call the Department of Motor Vehicles (DMV) for each state. The website addresses for each state's DMV are available in Appendix B.

The title should be at your local branch (or you should have arranged for it to be overnighted) as soon as the loan is paid off.

Get the transfer paperwork completed immediately, even if the vehicle won't be shipped straight away. Contact your DMV for help if you need it. If the funds are in escrow, fill out all the paperwork and file it as soon as the funds are released by the buyer.

When the Buyer Doesn't Pay

There are different reasons for nonpayment, and you resolve them differently. Whatever the reason, you should get the Transaction Fee refunded and become eligible for a Relist Credit if your item sells the second time.

Unfortunately though, you will not get any of your listing upgrade fees (for Bold, Highlight, Scheduled Listing, etc.) refunded.

To file for the fee credits, you will need to open an Unpaid Item Dispute. You'll need the auction item number, so write that down before you start.

1. Go to My eBay and click on Dispute Console.
2. Click Report an Unpaid Item.
3. Enter the item number.

Here's where it changes. You will have to select a reason for the dispute. Your two options are (1) the buyer has not paid for the item; or (2) we have both agreed not to complete the transaction. If you're using the latter option, you can file immediately, and assuming the buyer agrees when eBay contacts him, you will get the Final Value Fee Credit (also called Transaction Fee Credit) automatically applied to your account.

Detailing Tips

When you file a mutual withdrawal from transaction, the buyer will get an alert from eBay asking if he agreed to this. He must click yes. The instinct is to say no, but you must explain to the buyer that he needs to do this. If the buyer clicks no, you will not be eligible for the Final Value Fee Credit, and there is no appeal.

Now, if the buyer doesn't respond to your e-mails, you will need to file a full unpaid item dispute to get your fees credited. You have to wait seven days from the end of the auction to start this process (to allow time for the buyer to pay).

eBay will send the buyer an alert, and based on his response (or lack thereof), you should be able to close the dispute. If the buyer doesn't respond, you can close the dispute after seven days have passed. At that point, you will receive the Final Value Fee Credit.

Your options for closing a dispute are:

- **We've completed the transaction and we're both satisfied.** You won't get the Final Value Fee Credit because you will have completed the transaction and received payment from the buyer.

- **We've agreed not to complete the transaction.** The Final Value Fee Credit will be applied automatically.

- **I no longer wish to communicate with or wait for the buyer.** You have to wait seven days before using this option. This will put an unpaid item strike on the buyer's file at eBay as well as crediting you the Final Value Fee Credit.

You have 60 days from the end of the auction (not from when you first filed the dispute) to close an unpaid item dispute. If your time expires, the file will be closed automatically and you will not receive the Final Value Fee Credit. Nor will the buyer receive an unpaid item strike.

If the buyer doesn't respond to the alert from eBay and you close the dispute, he will not be allowed to leave feedback for you. However, you will be able to leave feedback for him. If the buyer does respond (even just to say "I'm not going to pay"), he is still eligible to leave feedback for you.

The Relist Credit

If your item doesn't sell, or your buyer backs out of the transaction, you may be eligible for a Relist Credit. This is not a refund of your Insertion fee. You must relist the item and only if it sells the second time will you receive a credit from eBay for one Insertion fee. You still pay it the second time, and it is credited to you if the item sells. However, if the item does not sell the second time, you will not get the credit, and you will end up having paid the Insertion fee for two auctions.

There are a few requirements to become eligible for the Relist Credit:

- You must be selling the exact same item.
- The starting price or Reserve price cannot be higher on the relist auction than on the original one.
- If you didn't use a Reserve price on the first auction, you cannot use one on the relist.
- You must use the Relist button on either the closed auction page or from the drop-down menu next to the item in My eBay.
- You must relist the item within 90 days.

Both the Final Value Fee Credit and the Relist Credit are there to help sellers from being too much out-of-pocket from a buyer who decides not to pay.

The Least You Need to Know

- If a vehicle is damaged after shipping, it is not your responsibility.

- Contact both your DMV and the DMV in the buyer's state to check what you need to do to transfer the title.

- You can file a mutual withdrawal from transaction form immediately after the auction ends, but if you are filing an Unpaid Item dispute, you must wait seven days.

- The Relist Credit is only available if the vehicle sells the second time.

Selling Parts and Accessories

In This Chapter

- Severely damaged or salvage vehicles
- Parts and Accessories fees
- Selling new or used parts
- Research tools for prices

You might think that only pristine vehicles sell on eBay. Wrong. Wrecked vehicles are hot items for parts or to be rebuilt. In this chapter, we look at how to sell wrecked vehicles as well as both new and used parts and accessories.

When Your Vehicle Doesn't Run

All types of people search eBay Motors for wrecked vehicles, so whether it has a salvage title or is just in serious need of restoration, you can still make a decent amount of money selling it on eBay Motors.

Driver's Ed

"Salvage," "Project Car," "Rebuildable," and "Wrecked" are four of the most searched terms on eBay Motors. I sold a wrecked vehicle last year and had more than 2,000 hits to the auction within three days.

If you are selling a damaged vehicle, you need to be extra vigilant with your description and be sure everything is disclosed. Take lots of photos—you should max out the 24-picture allowance. Get as much detail as you can of the damage. It's worth explaining what happened in the wreck, too. That helps the buyer determine how much damage there is (a 30-mile-an-hour crash will not usually impact the internal parts as much as a 60-mile-an-hour crash).

It's easy for an untrained eye to miss major damage (such as a twisted frame) that costs thousands to fix. So you may want to have a body shop or mechanic inspect it and give an estimate of repair costs. Be sure to include this in your description, but state that it is just an estimate from one body shop, and the actual repair cost could be higher.

If the vehicle has been declared a total loss by an insurance company, you'll likely have a report with detailed repair information. If you have this report, make it available to bidders so they can see the damage from a professional's viewpoint.

It makes a big difference if the car runs or not. If it can be driven onto a car-carrier, then the shipping cost will be far less than if it has to be winched. Use embedded video to prove it can be driven (see Chapter 9 for details on embedding video).

It's also worth showing a 360° tour of the vehicle so buyers can see exactly what is and is not damaged and put it in context. If it's not drivable, the video should also include the sound of the engine turning over. The sound will give an experienced rebuilder a lot of information that you can't put into words.

If you are not 100 percent certain of the vehicle's roadworthiness, do not let a buyer drive it away. Damage is often hidden, and even on a short trip could cause a catastrophe, and you could be legally liable. Specify that the damaged vehicle must be trailered or properly towed.

One thing you should strongly recommend is that the buyer personally, or a representative, comes to look at the vehicle. That way the buyer really understands the condition of the vehicle before bidding.

Selling Used Parts

If you've got the experience and facility to part out a wrecked vehicle, this is usually the way to go because you'll often make more money on the individual parts.

There are thousands of sellers who deal solely in used parts, and there is a huge market for it.

Driver's Ed

On most vehicle model-specific forums, there is a board for parts being sold. These are usually parts being replaced with an upgrade, but they sell like hot cakes. eBay is much the same way, but with a much wider audience.

Check the Completed Listings to see what the parts you're considering selling are really going for. If you have a lot of items to sell, it may be worth signing up for eBay Marketplace Research or Terapeak—both research tools show you the sales trends over the last few months. I talk about this later in the chapter.

Parts and Accessories Fees

The fee structure for Parts and Accessories is different from the rest of eBay Motors. It is aligned with the fees for the rest of eBay.

Listing Fees

For Parts and Accessories, the fees are called Insertion and Final Value fees.

Parts and Accessories Insertion Fees

Starting or Reserve Price	Insertion Fee
$0.01–$0.99	$0.20
$1.00–$9.99	$0.40
$10.00–$24.99	$0.60
$25.00–$49.99	$1.20
$50.00–$199.99	$2.40
$200.00–$499.99	$3.60
Over $500.00	$4.80

Parts and Accessories Final Value Fees

Tier	Final Selling Price	Final Value Fee
1	$0.01–$25.00	5.25% of the selling price
2	$25.01–$1,000.00	5.25% of the first $25; then 3.25% of the remaining balance
3	Over $1,000.01	5.25% of the first $25; then 3.25% of the value between $25.01 and $1,000; then 1.5% of the remaining balance

This may seem a little complicated. It's not once you get used to calculating it, but there is a great fee calculator at www.ebcalc.com that will do it for you (plus the optional listing fees if you want). It's one of the best fee calculators I've seen, and it's free.

Buy It Now

There is a minimal fee to offer a Buy It Now option on your auctions. To use Buy It Now you must:

- Have a feedback score of 10 or higher *or*
- Be ID Verified *or*
- Have a PayPal account and a feedback score of at least 5 and offer PayPal as a payment option on the auction

The fees are based on the Buy It Now price, not your starting or Reserve price.

Parts and Accessories Buy It Now Fees

Buy It Now Price	Fee
$0.01–$9.99	$0.05
$10.00–$24.99	$0.10
$25.00–$49.99	$0.20
Over $50.00	$0.25

Reserve Price Auction

The Reserve fee is based on the Reserve Price you set. This fee is fully refunded if the item sells.

Parts and Accessories Reserve Fees

Reserve Price	Fee
$0.01–$49.99	$1.00
$50.00–$199.99	$2.00

Reserve Price	Fee
Over $200.00 price (up to $50)	1% of the reserve

Listing Upgrades

Earlier I talked about listing upgrades and how they can be put to good use for the rest of eBay Motors. The good news is that the fees for Parts and Accessories are generally lower than for eBay Motors. Still, choose wisely.

You do have the option of using a subtitle (because you don't have the submodel box to complete). This is always worth paying for, as is the gallery. Other useful upgrades are Featured *Plus!* and Bold. Those are my favorites, but look at what is working in your category for similar items, and emulate that.

Parts and Accessories Listing Upgrade Fees

Listing Upgrade	Fee
Subtitle	$0.50
Gallery	$0.35
Gallery Plus	$0.75
Bold	$1.00
Border	$3.00
Highlight	$5.00
Listing Designer	$0.10
Scheduled Listing	$0.10

continues

Parts and Accessories Listing Upgrade Fees (continued)

Listing Upgrade	Fee
10-Day Duration	$0.40
Listing Icon	$1.00
Gallery Featured (includes Gallery)	$19.95
Featured *Plus!*	$19.95
Motors Home Page Featured	$24.95
Value Pack (Gallery, Listing Designer, and Subtitle)	$0.65
Pro Pack (Gallery Featured, Featured *Plus!*, Bold, Border, and Highlight)	$29.95

Don't forget that you can work out all your fees, including Final Value and PayPal fees, at www. ebcalc.com. There is a selection for Parts and Accessories, so you know the right fees will be used.

List in Two Categories

Parts and accessories can be listed in two categories simultaneously. Why would you do this? Well, let's say you're selling a die-cast model of a 1967 Chevy Camaro. You could list it in these two categories:

- **eBay Motors:** Parts and Accessories—Apparel and Merchandise—Car and Truck—Other Merchandise

- **eBay.com:** Toys and Hobbies—Die-Cast, Toy Vehicles—Cars, Trucks Die-Cast

Now you're getting twice the exposure for the item—to both buyers who are looking for collectibles for that car on eBay Motors, and those who know there is a die-cast category on eBay.com and are looking specifically there either for this model, or just for die-cast cars in general.

Use www.ebcalc.com to look at the difference in fees if you choose to list in two categories. Although you do pay double the Insertion Fee and most listing upgrade fees, you do not pay twice for Home Page Featured or Schedule Listing. Also, the Final Value Fee is only paid once, even if you list in two categories.

Selling New Parts or Accessories

There is also a huge market for new parts on eBay. Enthusiasts are constantly looking for ways to improve their vehicle and make it different from everyone else's. Remember what I said about getting the factory color right though. It's vitally important for painted parts.

When you take your photographs, you may want to do it outside to get natural light. Or use two lights to fill the photograph area. Wherever you choose to take the pictures, use a tripod (as I explained in Chapter 9).

You will also want a plain background. This can be as simple as a curved sheet of poster board or some paper laid out on the garage floor. But whatever you use, be sure it is clean and gives a good contrast to your part. For example, if your part is white or light silver, a dark background color is better than a light one.

As well as parts, there are accessories—shirts, patches, ball caps, key chains, watches, etc. There are thousands of merchandising opportunities. If you sell one particular manufacturer's parts, you should look into selling the same brand apparel.

Offer combined shipping, or send a discount coupon to your buyer in the end-of-auction e-mail good for a percentage off an apparel item purchased from you within the next 30 days. This helps get buyers looking at your other items if nothing else.

The Auctiva Scrolling Gallery

This is one of the most useful free tools you can add to your listings. Most parts and accessories sellers have multiple items for sale at the same time. So why not promote your other items within your auction description?

The really cool thing about Scrolling Gallery is that once you set it up, it is automatically added into all your auctions so you don't even have to think about it.

Scrolling Gallery is just as it sounds—it's a bar in your auction that displays the gallery thumbnail picture, plus the title, price, and time remaining for each of your active auctions. Five items are shown on each bar, and it scrolls to show other items you have for sale. The pictures are active links to the auctions, so buyers can click through to your other auctions very easily.

It's very easy to set up and doesn't cost you anything, so I highly recommend you do it. If you offer combined shipping, you'll find that helps increase the cross-sales, too. My cross-sales skyrocketed when I started using the Auctiva Scrolling Gallery.

Go to www.auctiva.com and sign up. It's free and doesn't take more than a couple minutes. You don't even need to put a credit card on file.

You do not have to use any of Auctiva's other auction management features. As long as the Scrolling Gallery is turned on (which should be automatic, but you can check in your Preferences), you can list your items using the eBay Sell Your Item form, or any other auction management program, and the Scrolling Gallery will display on all your auctions.

Parts and Accessories Research Tools

So how much is your item worth? You can look at the Completed Listings, but that only gives you data for a couple weeks. If you need more than that (which most sellers do) you have two options: Terapeak and eBay Marketplace Research.

Both are fee-based. Terapeak is a little more expensive, but it is one of the best research tools out there. Until recently, it was the only research tool to offer coverage for Parts and Accessories. This is called Motors P&A. It costs $24.95 per month for the basic subscription or $34.95 a month for the Pro version. That sounds like a lot, but if you're a high-volume seller, this saves you a lot of time and effort. Most people can get away with the regular version, but look at the features before you decide which to go for (terapeak.com/signup/compare_motors.php).

The biggest difference is that the Pro subscription gives you access to sales information for an entire year. The regular subscription gives you 30 days of data—twice what you get through Completed Listings.

Terapeak really is one of the pioneers of research tools. You can see all kinds of useful information, such as best times to list, best starting prices, average selling prices, sell-through rate, best category choices, as well as gauge your competition and seeing the sales trends over a period of time.

You can't get this from Completed Listings without doing a lot of time-consuming work. Frankly, how much is your time worth? $10 an hour, $20, more? How many hours do you think you would spend each month compiling this information through Completed Listings? All of a sudden, that $24.95 a month doesn't seem like so much after all.

Recently, eBay realized it was missing out on this market with its research tool (eBay Marketplace Research) so it has added a Parts and Accessories section, too. This is a little cheaper than Terapeak.

If you only have a few items to sell (such as if you're selling stock parts that you have replaced with upgrades), you should be able to use the Fast Pass. This gives you two days of access, but that should be more than enough for an occasional seller, and it's only $2.99. If you're selling more regularly, the Basic subscription ($9.99 a month) may be a better option. If you're a full-time seller, then the Pro subscription may be worth considering ($24.99 a month). The features vary for each subscription level. You can see a comparison at pages.ebay.com/marketplace_research/detailed-comparison.html.

Unfortunately, eBay keeps its vehicle sales information close to its chest so no research tools (not even its own) offer this data. You will only ever find Parts and Accessories included.

The Least You Need to Know

- There is a huge market for new and used vehicle parts on eBay.
- Wrecked vehicles are highly sought after for parting out or for rebuilding.
- Fees for Parts and Accessories are closer aligned with the rest of eBay than eBay Motors, which means they are generally lower.
- Increase your sales by cross-selling your items using the free Auctiva Scrolling Gallery.
- Use a research tool to find out the real sales trends for your item over a longer period of time.

Car Dealers on eBay Motors

In This Chapter

- When are you a dealer?
- Finding buyers in your Local Market
- Auction Management Programs
- Driving "traffic" to your website and dealership
- eBay University—Motors division

There are 15,000 registered dealers selling on eBay Motors. They wouldn't be there if it didn't make sound financial sense. In this chapter, we look at the additional programs available exclusively to dealers, as well as techniques that help you build your business.

Who's Considered a Dealer?

Different states have different requirements for becoming a dealer. Some require that you are specifically registered as a dealer, but others are based on volume. For example, if you sell more than three vehicles per year, in some states you would be considered a dealer.

As far as eBay is concerned, if you have a state-issued vehicle dealer license, you can register as a dealer on eBay.

First you must follow the steps previously discussed to register on eBay as a seller. Then you can register as a dealer. Go to ebay.carad.com/forms/dealerverification and complete the form.

> **Detailing Tips**
>
> You can register on eBay as a business rather than an individual. This allows you to authorize specific users for the account. These permissions can be modified as your employees change without affecting the rest of your account.

You need the information from your dealer license, as well as information about your General Manager or Dealer Principal, billing information, and additional information about your dealership and usual inventory.

Local Market Listings

Local Market is a new feature of eBay Motors. These listings are only visible to users searching within a 100-mile radius of your dealership.

Local Market listings are more like eBay Store listings although there is no Buy It Now price or even Starting Price. You list your sticker price and the buyer may make an offer, just like the Best Offer feature, but there is no actual Buy It Now button for the buyer to buy at the sticker price.

The two options a buyer has are Contact the Seller or Make Offer. You have the option to negotiate to an acceptable price, either in person or over the Internet. Once a buyer accepts your counteroffer, or you accept his, the listing ends. The listing runs for 30 days, but can be renewed at the end of that period if necessary.

The point of Local Market is to attract local buyers—those who can (and will) come and look at the vehicle in person and take a test drive. From the buyer's perspective, completing the transaction through eBay (after visiting your showroom) means the buyer is still eligible for Vehicle Purchase Protection and (if you are part of the program) Condition Guarantee by Seller.

Detailing Tips

It's smart to offer computer access to the buyer. This way, if you agree on a price, the buyer can immediately submit the offer and you can accept it and close the deal. If the buyer leaves the dealership, you're more likely to lose the sale.

When you first sign up as a dealer with eBay Motors, you are assigned a Dealer Consultant for the first 90 days. If you show good growth and are selling vehicles (closed through eBay), you may be handed over to a Top-Seller Account Manager (TSAM). After a time, the TSAM may decide that your record and volume warrant an invitation to participate in the Condition Guarantee by Seller program. This is done on a case-by-case basis, so there are no guarantees that you will be selected for this program.

Local Market Costs

Local Market was designed for dealers with a lot of inventory. You pay a flat-rate $1,000 a month to list as many vehicles as you want in this format. The idea is to get your entire dealership inventory online. You must use one of eBay Motors' Preferred Solution Providers, and they also have fees (ranging from about $15 per listing to $299 for unlimited use).

That might sound like a lot, but first consider how many actual buyers visit your dealership each month. Maybe 1,000 if you've got a good location? On eBay Motors, there are 12 million unique visitors online each month and a passenger vehicle sells every 60 seconds. So you can see that the market and buyers are there.

But what about the cost? If you choose to use the unlimited listing from one of eBay's Preferred Solution Providers, you pay about $300 a month. So add that to the monthly fee from eBay and you've got $1,300. That's $1,300 to list every vehicle you have on your lot on eBay for 30 days.

How much are you paying per month for print advertising? How many loss leaders do you use to get buyers onto the lot? I would bet money that your costs are more than $1,300 a month.

Your print advertising only targets the readers of that particular magazine or newspaper, so you have to advertise in many newspapers, incurring more and more cost to you. But wait, eBay Motors is used by millions of buyers. Here you list the ad, you pay monthly, not weekly, and you will see a significant return on your investment.

Dollar for dollar, Local Market is a much better deal than any other form of advertising. Plus, you can probably get away with a mini-commission for your sales force because you may well do the negotiation part over the Internet yourself. That alone can save you thousands.

You can read more by downloading the Local Market brochure at pages.ebay.com/motors/services/dealer_center/eBay_Motors_Local_Market.pdf.

Document Fees

Some states mandate document fee charges (referred to as a "doc" fee), and others don't. You can still charge the document fee as an "add on" after the final price is determined. Just be sure to be very specific about the amount in the description. Most buyers don't realize that this fee is often state-enforced, so they think it is an extra profit center for the dealership. Be specific about the amount and explain that it is state mandated (if it is).

If it isn't a state-required fee, then you have a bit more flexibility. You can choose to charge the full amount as usual, or you can use it as a way to entice buyers. "No Doc Fees" is a great bonus to entice buyers.

About Me Page

Your About Me Page is the only place you can put a link to your dealership website. An impressive page lends you credibility, and you may get some buyers clicking through to your website and buying directly from you.

Check Engine

If a buyer contacts you through My Messages, rather than e-mailing you through your web form on your own website, then you need to treat it as an eBay sale. Also, you must never suggest to a buyer that you conduct the transaction off eBay. This is a direct violation of eBay's terms and conditions and can land you in trouble with account limitations, loss of PowerSeller status, and possibly even suspension. It's just not worth it for the sake of $50.

Don't forget that if you registered as a business, your eBay fees become a business marketing expense that you can write off come tax time.

Auctioning Vehicles

How much would you make at a vehicle auction for one of your used vehicles? Don't expect to get Blue Book retail, but you can get close, and the commission is far less. The most successful sellers treat eBay as their liquidation source for used vehicles, but they also realize higher prices for late-model vehicles.

Many dealers choose to run some of their vehicles in the auction format in addition to using Local Market. This is because the auction listings have higher visibility because they are not limited to shoppers within 100 miles of your dealership. With the wider visibility, you can use auctions to draw attention to your other inventory—vehicles that are only listed as Local Listings.

Also, Local Market listings are only for late-model cars and trucks. If you're selling older or other types of vehicles, you need to run those as Online Auctions or Fixed Price listings anyway.

Unusual, collectible, or No Reserve vehicles draw a lot of attention and pull eyeballs toward your more mundane inventory. Keep a few auctions running at all times to expand your local market to a national market.

You can choose to run your auction for a variety of durations, but the most common seems to be seven-day auctions.

Detailing Tips

eBay traffic spikes on weekends, so most dealers try to be sure their listings run over at least one weekend to get the most traffic.

What If It Doesn't Sell?

If an auction vehicle doesn't sell the first time, you can relist it and if it sells the second time (and if you followed the proper process I outlined in Chapter 13), you should be eligible for the Relist Credit. This refunds one of the Insertion fees you paid. So you essentially got a free relist.

One of the great reasons to use eBay Motors is that it doesn't matter where you are, someone will be interested in the vehicle. If your dealership is in New York and you get a 2005 Mazda Miata traded in during the winter months, you might think it will sit on your lot until the snow clears and the weather improves. Not so with eBay Motors.

There are people in Florida and other southern states searching for a good deal on just that type of vehicle year round. Frankly, winter is a good time for them to buy a convertible because they can actually use it before the humidity gets oppressive.

You won't have to negotiate as much with these buyers, and you will get far more for the vehicle than you could hope to realize in your own state at that time of year.

What If It Sells on My Lot?

If your vehicle sells before the auction duration is up, you can end your listing early. The option to use is "Item is no longer available for sale." You should specify in your auction description that all eBay listings are subject to cancellation based on local sale. Most buyers assume this, but it never hurts to reiterate it.

The only thing to watch for is the "last 12 hour rule." This states that you cannot cancel an auction with bids during the last 12 hours if the Reserve Price has been met (or you have a bid on a no-reserve auction).

So either you need to cancel the auction before those last 12 hours if you have someone interested in the vehicle locally, or you need to hide the vehicle so potential local buyers can't see it until the auction has ended (just in case you get a last-minute bid).

What Not to Do in Your Listings

I've seen some examples of dealerships with unfair descriptions. They say "flawless paint" and then in a paragraph in the terms and conditions state that "usual wear and tear associated with used vehicles including dents, dings, scratches, rust, etc. may be present and undisclosed." This is unfair to the buyer and is really a form of misrepresentation. The seller is including two different conditions and hoping that the buyer misses the second reference.

Another thing you mustn't do is bid on your own auctions. This is called *shill bidding* and will get you suspended from eBay and possibly fined by the government.

def•i•ni•tion

Shill bidding is bidding on an item without the intention of actually buying it. Usually this is done to artificially raise the price of an item.

Also, do not think you can ask a friend in a distant town to bid up your item. It may work once, but in the end you'll get caught. It's just not worth it. eBay has some very sophisticated tools to catch shill bidders, and it uses them.

Your feedback score is incredibly important. Don't do anything that could taint it. Put on your best marketing hat to work on the wording for your description to make it as persuasive as possible, but always be sure it is accurate and factual.

Don't stretch the truth. Most buyers label you as dishonest as soon as they catch it and move on to another seller. So in the long run it hurts your sales, not helps them.

Don't put your terms and conditions exclusively on your About Me Page. This is not the place to hide document fees or other fees you wish to charge in addition to the final selling price. Those should be clearly disclosed in the auction description.

You can put them on your About Me Page as well (to show you have nothing to hide), but if you don't include them in your listing description as well, your buyers may think you are trying to hide additional fees or terms and conditions that should have been easier to find.

CARad

I mentioned CARad and CARad Express in Chapter 11. eBay purchased CARad a few years ago, but it still offers the same auction management services for eBay Motors.

CARad is specifically for dealerships and offers features you will likely use, such as inventory management reports, My Garage to showcase your entire inventory, links for frequently asked questions, e-mail management for improved buyer communication, listing templates, and a unique way of displaying all your photos with a zoom-in feature (very popular with buyers). You also get to upload 35 pictures instead of the maximum 24 available through eBay's Picture Services. CARad costs $9.95 per listing, or $299 for unlimited monthly use.

Getting Further Assistance

If you need help getting registered as a dealer, you can contact an eBay Motors Dealer Consultant at 1-866-MOTORS4 (1-866-668-6774). If you have already registered and need help with any other aspect of selling on eBay Motors, you can call 1-866-EBAYCAR (1-866-322-9227).

There is also a Dealer Center on eBay Motors that you can access to read more information about programs and see tips and tricks from the pros. To get to the Dealer Center:

1. Click Sell on the navigation bar at the top right of the page.
2. Scroll down to the Selling Resources box at the bottom of the page and click Dealer Center.

Alternatively, you can go directly to pages.motors. ebay.com/services/dealer_center/dealer_center.html.

Seminars and Independent Consultations

eBay University offers online classes for specific areas of eBay Motors (such as how to use CARad). Throughout the year, eBay Motors also offers live seminars at various locations around the country.

Steve Lindhorst (who I am very lucky to have as the technical editor for this book) is eBay University's resident eBay Motors expert. If you've attended one of eBay University's Motors live seminars, Steve might have been running it. He also speaks to state dealer associations and 20 Groups around the country. He's been doing this since 2004, so he really knows his stuff.

Steve's work with dealerships is two-fold. Besides instructing for eBay University and other organizations, he also works with individual dealerships as an independent consultant.

He works with you to figure out your specific goals for the eBay side of your business and then sets you up with a plan to get you there.

He trains you in the nuts and bolts of creating your eBay Motors listings; expectations of eBay Motors buyers and how to communicate with them; developing and fine-tuning your selling strategy; and which eBay and third-party tools get you the best bang for your buck. His consultation fee includes six months of follow-up via phone or e-mail, so you aren't left on your own after the initial training.

There are very few true eBay Motors experts, and even fewer that really understand the inner workings of dealerships. Steve Lindhorst is one of them. He has hands-on experience selling for dealerships, so he really does "get it."

You can read more about what Steve does at www.dealerclasses.com. You can also reach him via e-mail at steve@dealerclasses.com or via phone at 805-286-8283.

The Least You Need to Know

- Don't expect to get sticker price, but you'll usually get "whole-tail" (between wholesale and retail) for your used vehicles.

- Always clearly disclose any damage, whether it is rust, dings, dents, scratches, tears, or any other damage.

- You can end an auction if you sell the vehicle locally, but only if 12 hours remain on your auction.

- Use Local Market to locate buyers in your area through a nonauction format listing.

- If in doubt, take advantage of an expert who works solely with dealerships selling on eBay Motors.

Glossary

About Me Page A page on eBay that sellers can create all about them. Dealers can use it to promote their dealership. This page is the only place you can put an off-eBay link.

Best Offer An option sellers can add to a Fixed Price listing to let buyers offer a lower amount for the seller's consideration. Sellers can accept, reject, or counter a Best Offer.

Buy It Now An option for auctions that allows the first buyer to purchase the item for a higher, fixed price rather than place a starting bid. The Buy It Now price usually disappears after the first bid over the Reserve price is placed.

CARad An auction management company for eBay Motors dealers. This includes auction templates and picture hosting as well as inventory management. CARad is for dealers only.

CARad Express The version of CARad designed for individual sellers. It doesn't include as much of the inventory management side, but does include the templates and picture hosting services.

Completed Listings   A section of eBay that shows listings that have ended within the last two weeks. The prices in green are for items that sold. Those in red did not sell (if there were bids, the price did not reach the Reserve price).

Condition Guarantee by Seller   A program for high-volume vehicle dealers that guarantees their item descriptions to be accurate. This builds credibility and trust with potential buyers.

Detailed Seller Ratings   A one- to five-star rating from buyers based on four areas of the transaction. These do not show up on your feedback profile until you have 10 responses from buyers.

escrow   A payment transfer service. The buyer pays the escrow company, the seller ships the vehicle to the buyer, and the buyer instructs the escrow company to release the funds to the seller. This is one of the securest methods of payment, but only if you use a genuine escrow company like www.escrow.com.

Fixed Price listing   A listing with no starting price. There is only the fixed price (also called the Buy It Now price). There are no bids, only purchases.

Giving Works   eBay's charity program used for donating a portion of your final selling price to the charity of your choice. eBay credits you the same portion of your eBay Insertion and Final Value fees. So if you donate 15 percent, you get 15 percent of your fees back. The minimum donation is $5.00.

guides   How-to information written by eBay users. For example, one guide might teach you how to replace the exhaust system on your vehicle.

ID Verify   Third-party service that verifies your identity using information from your credit history. The service costs $5.00 and is valid until you change your address or phone number.

Item Specifics   Details about your item that eBay uses when buyers narrow down their search results.

Listing Designer   An option for adding a border around your item description and changing the layout of the text and pictures on the page.

My eBay   The hub of your eBay transactions. Here you will find a list of all the items you are watching, bidding on, have bought, have sold, or have listed for sale. You also access your eBay e-mails and personal details here.

My Messages   eBay's e-mail system. eBay users can e-mail each other through My Messages without giving out their personal e-mail address.

PayPal   eBay's online payment processing system. It allows sellers to accept credit cards without having a merchant credit card account and allows buyers to pay with a credit card without giving their card details to the seller. Buyers can also pay through PayPal by bank transfer.

PayPal Confirmed Address   You have added a credit card to your account. PayPal confirms that the billing address for the credit card matches the information you registered with, hence confirming your address is accurate.

PayPal Expanded Use Program   One of two options for removing the withdrawal limit on your PayPal account. You verify a code next to a $1.95 charge PayPal makes to your card. The fee is refunded after you make your next PayPal payment.

PayPal Instant Transfer   An immediate transfer of funds from one PayPal account to another. It can be used only if the funds to cover the transaction are already in the sender's account, or the sender has both a credit card and a bank account on file with PayPal.

PayPal Verified   You have added a bank account to your PayPal account and PayPal has verified that you are the owner (by depositing two small amounts that you had to confirm).

PowerSeller   A seller who sells at least $1,000 a month on eBay, maintains a 98 percent feedback rating, and has a feedback score of 100 or more. eBay is also setting up a way for high-volume, low-value sellers to become PowerSellers, but the details have not yet been released.

Reserve Price   A hidden amount the seller can set that is the lowest he will sell the item for. This is hidden so he can start the bidding lower to build interest in the auction, but still protect himself from having to sell the vehicle for lower than he can afford.

reviews   Product reviews written by eBay users. This could be a review for anything from a K&N Cold Air Intake, to a particular model year vehicle.

Second Chance Offer   If the highest bidder backs out of the transaction, the bidding doesn't reach the Reserve, or the seller has an identical item for sale not currently at auction, he may send a Second Chance Offer to any of the nonwinning bidders. For eBay Motors vehicle auctions, the seller may increase the Second Chance Offer amount up to, but not over, his Reserve price. For parts and accessories, the Second Chance Offer is for the highest bid that bidder placed.

Sell Your Item form   Used to list your item on eBay. Get to it by clicking Sell on the main navigation bar (top right of every eBay Motors page).

Terapeak   A third-party company that offers research tools for eBay as well as eBay Motors Parts and Accessories (www.terapeak.com).

vehicle history report   A report through CARFAX or AutoCheck that shows the history of the vehicle. Information includes the number of owners, rental/fleet car, major damage or repairs, salvage/junk/rebuilt title, possible flood damage, etc.

Vehicle Identification Number (VIN)   The Social Security number of your vehicle. Everything to do with your vehicle is reported with the VIN. Vehicle history reports are linked to the VIN. You can find this number under the hood and on the dashboard (and they should match).

Vehicle Protection Program   The fraud-protection program for eBay Motors vehicle buyers. This includes both Vehicle Purchase Protection and Condition Guarantee by Seller.

Vehicle Purchase Protection   The main eBay
Motors fraud-protection program. It covers buyers
for up to $20,000 or the cost of the vehicle, which-
ever is lower. This is exclusive to eBay Motors.

Verified buyer   eBay user who has added a credit
or debit card to their eBay account to verify their
identity. This is required for all buyers wishing to
place a bid over $15,000.

VeRO   eBay's copyright protection program. It
stands for Verified Rights Owner. If your auction
is tagged as a VeRO violation, it will likely be can-
celed by eBay and you will not receive a refund on
your fees. You will likely get an official warning as
well. Too many VeRO violations, and you will be
suspended.

Appendix B

Resources

Department of Motor Vehicles

State Department of Motor Vehicles (DMV) Websites

Alabama	www.ador.state.al.us/motorvehicle/index.html
Alaska	www.state.ak.us/dmv
Arizona	www.azdot.gov/mvd
Arkansas	www.state.ar.us/dfa/dfa_vehicles.html
California	www.dmv.ca.gov
Colorado	www.revenue.state.co.us/mv_dir/home.asp
Connecticut	dmvct.org
Delaware	www.dmv.de.gov
Florida	www.hsmv.state.fl.us
Georgia	www.dds.ga.gov
Hawaii	www.hawaii.gov/dot/publicaffairs/motorvehicleregistration.htm
Idaho	itd.idaho.gov
Illinois	www.sos.state.il.us

continues

State Department of Motor Vehicles (DMV) Websites (continued)

Indiana	www.state.in.us/bmv
Iowa	www.dot.state.ia.us/mvd
Kansas	www.ksrevenue.org/vehicle.htm
Kentucky	www.kytc.state.ky.us/mvl
Louisiana	omv.dps.state.la.us
Maine	www.maine.gov/sos/bmv
Maryland	www.mva.state.md.us
Massachusetts	www.mass.gov/rmv
Michigan	www.michigan.gov/sos
Minnesota	www.dps.state.mn.us/dvs
Mississippi	www.mmvc.state.ms.us
Missouri	dor.mo.gov/mvdl
Montana	doj.mt.gov/driving
Nebraska	www.dmv.state.ne.us
Nevada	www.dmvnv.com
New Hampshire	www.state.nh.us/dmv
New Jersey	www.nj.gov/mvc
New Mexico	www.tax.state.nm.us/mvd
New York	www.nydmv.state.ny.us
North Carolina	www.ncdot.org/dmv
North Dakota	www.dot.nd.gov
Ohio	bmv.ohio.gov
Oklahoma	www.dps.state.ok.us
Oregon	www.oregon.gov/odot/dmv
Pennsylvania	www.dot.state.pa.us
Rhode Island	www.dmv.state.ri.us

State Department of Motor Vehicles (DMV) Websites

South Carolina	www.scdmvonline.com
South Dakota	www.state.sd.us/drr2/motorvehicle
Tennessee	www.state.tn.us/safety
Texas	www.dot.state.tx.us
Utah	dmv.utah.gov
Vermont	www.aot.state.vt.us/dmv
Virginia	www.dmv.state.va.us
Washington	www.dol.wa.gov
Washington, D.C.	www.dmv.washingtondc.gov
West Virginia	www.wvdot.com
Wisconsin	www.dot.state.wi.us
Wyoming	dot.state.wy.us

eBay Pages

eBay Motors	www.motors.ebay.com
eBay Motors fees	pages.ebay.com/help/sell/motorfees.html
Vehicle Protection Program	pages.motors.ebay.com/services/overview.html
General announcements	www2.ebay.com/aw/marketing.shtml?_trksid=m37
System announcements	www2.ebay.com/aw/announce.shtml

eBay Motors discussion board	forums.ebay.com/db1/forum.jspa?forumID=20
Feedback forum	pages.ebay.com/services/forum/feedback.html
DMV websites	pages.motors.ebay.com/help/dmv.html

Shipping Companies

Express Auto Transport
1-800-209-5042
www.theexpressauto.com

United Road
1-866-608-6277
www.vehicletransportusa.com

Dependable Auto Shippers
1-800-827-6998
www.DASautoshippers.com

Reviews about auto shipping companies
www.transportreviews.com

Vehicle Research

Edmunds	www.Edmunds.com
Kelley Blue Book	www.KBB.com
NADA Guides	www.NadaGuides.com
Black Book	www.Blackbook.com

Index

G

H–I–J

T

W-X-Y-Z